GREENWICH LIBRARIES

3 8028 01075153 2

D0657771

ENGLAND'S HERITAGE

Book of
Canterbury

ENGLISH ❖ HERITAGE

Book of
Canterbury

Marjorie Lyle

B. T. Batsford Ltd/English Heritage
London

GREENWICH LIBRARIES

FOR LAWRENCE

and

in piam memoriam

WILLIAM GEORGE URRY

1913–1981

City and Cathedral Archivist

GREENWICH LIBRARIES   LOC WO

INV   S1   25/11/94   £14.99

ACC NO   3 8028 01075153 2

CAT   942.234

REFERENCE

© Marjorie Lyle 1994

First published 1994

All rights reserved. No part of this publication
may be reproduced, in any form or by any means,
without permission from the Publisher

Typeset by Lasertext Ltd, Stretford, Manchester
and printed in Great Britain by
The Bath Press, Bath

Published by B T Batsford Ltd
4 Fitzhardinge Street, London W1H 0AH

A CIP catalogue record for this book is
available from the British Library

ISBN 0 7134 7314 2 (cased)
0 7134 7315 0 (limp)

Contents

Illustrations

Colour Plates

Introduction

Canterbury's written and architectural resources have been closely studied for over a century, and the national personalities associated with the city, like Becket and Marlowe, are still hotly debated. Its archaeology is more recent and in both quantity and quality stretches the post-excavation resources of a small unit. Comparative urban studies of economy, society and demography are also relatively new. It would be impossible to draw these strands together in a short work without the generous help of many with specialist knowledge much greater than my own; remaining errors, escaping their scrutiny, are my responsibility. Like the shifting coastline of Kent itself, judgements have so often changed with growing knowledge, during my forty years' residence, that I am aware that my statements will be a snapshot of current thinking, rather than the final word.

Paul Bennett, Director of the Archaeological Trust, examined all matters Roman and archaeological, while his predecessor, Tim Tatton-Brown, scrutinized the Norman chapter and gave freely of his architectural advice. Margaret Sparks, editor of the forthcoming Cathedral history, was equally helpful over the Saxon chapter and matters ecclesiastical. Margaret Fisher generously shared her researches into the Walloons and Huguenots, and Dr Frank Panton his on the eighteenth-century city. I learned much about the medieval and Tudor communities from Andrew Butcher of the University of Kent at Canterbury.

Practical help has abounded from Harry Mountford over maps; for pictures from David Cousins of the Canterbury Reference Library and Neil Mattingly for prints. Of the Trust staff, Nigel MacPherson-Grant and Andrew Savage have guided me over pottery, Rupert Austin over buildings and Adrian Murphy has done the extra photography, while without Simon Pratt the illustrations would not have come together. Clive Barham reconstructed the Bronze Age vessels.

To the students of my WEA class I owe a special debt, particularly to Kenneth Pinnock and Mrs Kate Urry. Many are City and Cathedral guides, or long-term residents, whose specialist knowledge and keen interest tax my presentational skills. Much of this material was tried out on them and their response encourages me to hope that, if they are happy, the book will fill a need and still be readable. Without my husband's word-processing skills, grammatical acumen and moral support it would never have been completed at all.

All maps are based on OS 1874, except where permission has been granted but ascribed to and reserved by the Ordnance Survey as Crown Copyright (**1**, **13** and **74**).

All drawings and photographs were prepared by Canterbury Archaeological Trust or myself except where copyright is retained by the following, for whose permission to reproduce them I am grateful:

53 John Atherton Bowen, whose work for the Trust speaks for itself in many reconstructions here.

1 and **74** Harry Mountford

13 Dr Alec Detsicas

35 English Heritage

16 and **19** and **back cover** Canterbury Royal Museums

77 Kent County Library, Local History room, Canterbury.

Colour plate 12 and **82** and **83** University of Kent at Canterbury

Colour plates 10 and **11** and **67** Neil Mattingly

66 and **76** Paul Crampton (Fisk-Moore Studio Collection)

12 Brian Stewart.

36 and **Colour plate 5**, the photograph of the Saxon Cathedral, appear with the kind permission of the Dean and Chapter; **colour plate 8b** through the cooperation of Mr R Steele of Cathedral Gifts Ltd; **8a** through the cooperation of the Museum of London.

1

Image and origins

Say Canterbury to a stranger and the word pilgrim inevitably follows. This little East Kent market town carries a load of expectation and a resonance disproportionate to its size and function. The idea of Canterbury and the debt owed to its long history has, in times of strife and death, often driven people to behave in ways larger than life, whether archbishops like Alphege and Becket, humble Protestant martyrs, puritan iconoclasts or firefighters in the blitz. Like a magnet, it has attracted architects of genius, barefoot friars and skilled religious refugees; drawn back or retained native sons like Sidney Cooper, the artist, or William Somner, the antiquarian; evoked comments from visitors as diverse as Erasmus and Marx. Some, like Christopher Marlowe, it sensitized but did not hold.

When Augustine and his monks arrived in 597, chanting 'Let Thy anger and wrath be turned away from this city', they already believed it an ancient place, to be recovered for Christianity. Its renown as the repository of famous and holy bones was old when Becket's murder and Henry II's penance set the seal on its European status as a shrine. This inheritance drove medieval archbishops, monks and kings to wrangle over Canterbury's primacy and rights. After the Reformation, 'this Antient City' guarded as jealously its independence from Kent, 'for ever', and its parliamentary status. Nineteenth-century councillors adopted the motto '*Ave Mater Angliae*', 'Hail Mother

of England'; Canterbury remained England's smallest County Borough until 1974 and successfully retains its Lord Mayor today. One of the Cathedral archive's treasures is the Accord of Winchester of 1072, bearing the Conqueror's mark and witnessed by Lanfranc and his fellow bishops, in which the Archbishop of York conceded the Archbishop of Canterbury's right to be Primate of all England, as he still is today. To this role is added leadership of the world-wide Anglican Communion. The city of pilgrims could be likened to Jerusalem in its downfall, by Lambarde; be visited, 'on pilgrimage, but by train', by Kilvert, but only Chaucer, by a stroke of genius, stopped short before his pilgrims arrived. The illusions of the Miller, Pardoner and Wife of Bath about their goal could remain intact, whether about the quality of the beer or the business and matrimonial prospects ahead.

Like any living organism, the city has adapted to recurrent disasters – at the end of the Roman period, under Viking attack, at the Dissolution of the Monasteries and in the Second World War. Periods of prosperity created a legacy of magnificent buildings, but as important were periods of standstill, in the later Middle Ages, the seventeenth, nineteenth and early twentieth centuries, which preserved this legacy relatively intact. For this reason visitors and citizens value Canterbury's beauty and its contrasts of scale. Ruskin, returning from Venice, was less complimentary about 'the doll's house look of the principal street . . . the peculiar, red-bricked, smooth-shaven yet old-fashioned simplicity of smallness, the perfection of Establishment, . . . one cannot conceive anybody living in Canterbury to have any ideas of advance or change or anything in the world out of Canterbury'. The city's spell was marvellously described, in 1924, by Cunninghame Grahame:

> the houses with their casement windows, timbered upper storeys, and overhanging eaves, still kept the air of an older world. The gateways with their battlements and low archways, through which the medieval traffic once had flowed . . . to the shrine of Becket, were now mere monuments. Grouped round its dominating church, the city huddled as if it sought protection against progress and modernity. Bell Harry in his beauty pointed heavenwards. It was indeed a haven.

Today's citizens have faced post-war rebuilding, torrents of tourists and the redevelopment boom of the 1980s, while trying to retain, not just the image of red roofs clustered around the shining Cathedral, but a real small town, growing from and serving its neighbourhood. The *Architectural Journal* of 1952 was scathing about 'a city of contradictory citizens who want to rebuild without renewing, replace without destroying and revolutionize without revolting'. Whether 1950s' 'brave new world' shops, the 1960s' Christchurch College and University, or the backward-looking styles of the 1980s, in a setting of lovingly restored medieval buildings, shows this to be unkind, curious visitors must decide for themselves.

Canterbury has many guidebooks but few histories. The last polymath able to do the city justice, Dr William Urry, died in 1981, working on such a book, which he had promised to himself in 1932. In his preface to Somner's *Antiquities of Canterbury* Urry wrote, 'perhaps the enormous wealth of Canterbury in terms of architecture, archaeology, manuscripts, archives and chronicles is enough to deter

would-be writers of any general account'. While pacing the High Street, avoiding the site of a fifteenth-century bollard, he would quote from Somner's biography, 'his visits within the city were to find out the Ancestors rather than the present inhabitants and to know the genealogy of houses, walls and dust . . . the British bricks, the Roman ways, the Danish hills, the Saxon monasteries and the Norman churches'.

This short archaeological survey is not the work these men could write, but a small tribute to William Urry, who taught me to see rather than to look and to walk not just in space but in time. The Canterbury Archaeological Trust, which he supported keenly, was only six years old at his death. Since then, it has revolutionized our knowledge of Canterbury's first 1500 years and analysed its standing architectural legacy as the illustrations reveal. This book is also a tribute to the work of its first two Directors and their staff without whose help it could not have been written.

Site, geology and geography

Canterbury's situation in East Kent is both *en route* from the Continent to London and isolated, being surrounded on three sides by sea and, until recently, cut off on the fourth by the forested Weald. It is easier to communicate with the continent of Europe than with Britain beyond London, but, throughout two millennia and more, invaders have had to negotiate this spot at the foot of the North Downs dip-slope, where East Kent's only major river flows from the Stour gap eastwards to the sea. Modern 'A' roads follow the Roman pattern which made the city the hub of a road wheel connecting their coastal forts from 9 to 16 miles away.

The original riverbank settlement (**1**) is buried deep by two thousand years of building, demolition, decay and reconstruction. Brick earth overlying river gravels is found about 2m (6ft) down in the centre, while Roman levels below the alluvium near the river are now 0.61m (2ft) below the present water-table. Low

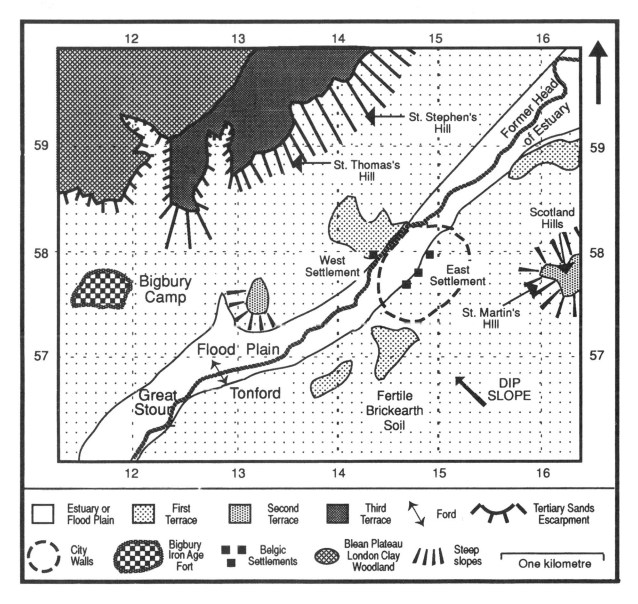

| | Estuary or Flood Plain | | First Terrace | | Second Terrace | | Third Terrace | | Ford | | Tertiary Sands Escarpment |
| | City Walls | | Bigbury Iron Age Fort | | Belgic Settlements | | Blean Plateau London Clay Woodland | | Steep slopes | | One kilometre |

river terraces, north-east and south-west of the site, provided a possible early crossing point, since the wide flood plain upstream is still liable to flooding and the gravel workings and lakes downstream were probably the former head of the Stour estuary. Tertiary Thanet sands create a middle terrace on the eastern slopes of St Martin's and Scotland hills, whence monks, and probably Romans before them, drew their pure water. St Stephen's and St Thomas' hills to the north-west are Tertiary sands overlain by London clay. This cold earth, on the edge

1 *A map of the geology of the Canterbury area. Although the precise location of the early ford is unknown, settlement occurred up to and during the Roman period on both sides of it. The surviving line of the 270 city wall shows how the western suburb was then excluded.*

of Blean woods, made poor farmland and is now the site of the University. Surrounded by such varied geology and forming a focus of communications, Canterbury has always been an exchange centre for a whole range of agricultural produce, fish, and sea and riverborne imports.

Flint and chalk provide the local stone; Kentish ragstone, coastal greensands, Caen and Quarr stone and, later, brick came up-river, although tiles were locally produced. This shortage of local building materials meant everything was reused, as St Peter's Church tower clearly shows. Robber trenches leave archaeologists only the ghosts of former buildings, like the Roman theatre, and after Henry VIII took the best Caen stone for his castles, the citizens rapidly reduced St Augustine's great Abbey church to the ground.

Early migrants and occupants

The Stour gravel terraces have yielded a good number of lower palaeolithic implements, particularly ovate handaxes. Most appeared round Sturry, where the river may have washed them towards the estuary. At Canterbury, the western bank in St Dunstan's produced over 30, on two sites, some of advanced technique. On the 70m (230ft) contour above St Thomas' hill, three particularly fine handaxes appeared in disturbed ground. Living and working sites may be found, but these tools seem to belong to migrants, making their way along higher ground above the alder swamps. A neolithic pot and other sherds of Ebbsfleet type dated from 3000 BC were found on the west bank of the Stour underneath Roman Watling Street (**3**).

Canterbury's earliest Bronze Age pot, dating to 1400–1000 BC, was found at Christchurch College, below the St Martin's north-eastern terrace. Made of flint-tempered clay with lug handles, it appears to have been designed to take a cover of fabric or wood and was in refuse from an occupation site with post-holes and pits. Recently, an enclosure with a ditch and perhaps palisade at St John's Lane has been linked, by comparative pottery studies, to the Trust's first excavation at Highstead, near Chislet. At the transition from Bronze to Iron age, around 900–600 BC, a strong and quite uniform pottery tradition flourished, here and elsewhere. An important ford, at this spot on the North Downs trackway, was obviously already established. After a gap, pottery with continental affinities reappears, about 550–300 BC, followed by another hiatus. Pottery suggests reoccupation, perhaps twenty years before Caesar's first visit in 55 BC. Since the same area of today's city was successively recolonized in each phase, a regular ford must have existed. When the Belgic *oppidum* grew, again in this location, in the century between Caesar and Claudius, native Iron Age ware gave way to the superior products of the new immigrants.

From Caesar to Claudius

Caesar's description of East Kent's inhabitants, so like his Gaulish adversaries, reveals a densely settled farming people, whose long-haired warriors used war chariots and differed from the hunting and pastoral people of West Kent. His spirited account of his 54 BC campaign, when he stormed a hillfort in wooded country above a ford, probably refers to nearby Bigbury. Chance finds and quarrying there revealed, besides pottery, metalwork for agriculture, forestry, carpentry, horse management and slave trading. The latest exploration suggests that the settlement was abandoned around 50 BC, after which a major township began to grow at Durovernon. A similar migration from Quarry Wood hillfort to Rochester seems to be contemporary.

During the next century, other valley-side townships grew in lowland Britain, where trade routes crossed rivers, and here both terrace banks of the Stour were settled (**4**). The larger south-eastern concentration was defended by complex triple ditches with offset entrances showing evidence of regular recutting and maintenance. A road in from the south, when excavated, retained thin wheel ruts and the hoofprints of many animals (**5**). Round huts with porched entrances have been found spread in groups from the area round Watling Street to the Longmarket (**2**). There is some evidence

2 *Belgic hut reconstruction. Several circular huts were found within the defences, all levelled about AD 70 for the first Roman buildings. This example, with a porched entrance, had been re-sited and contained a cremation urn, a hearth with bronze slag, and a scatter of potin coins, native pottery and stake-holes.*

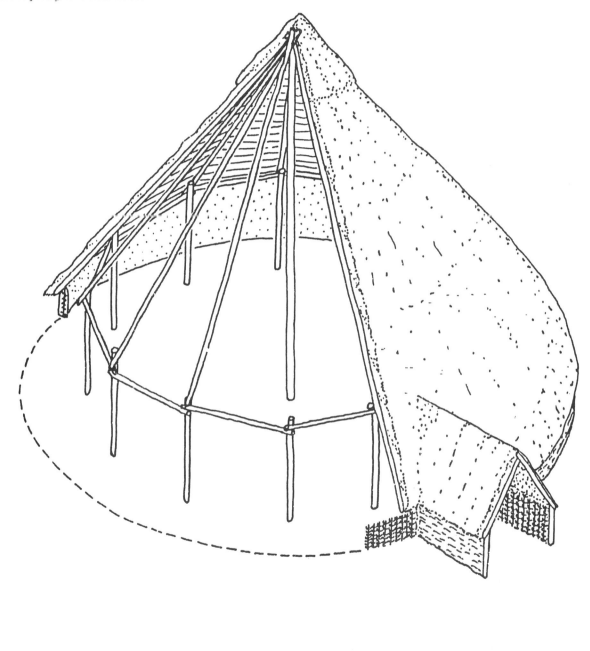

0   5
M

for a new fashion for squarish huts in the later period. The craftspeople of the settlement were spinning and weaving, manufacturing in bronze and iron and cooking in wheel-thrown pots on tiled hearths. Native pottery was joined by imported Roman *amphorae*, red and black vessels and Arretine platters and imitative wares coming from Camulodunum (Colchester) (**6**).

Coinage may have started with payments to warriors aiding the Gauls against Rome, but soon became more common. Potin coins of Cunobelin, the Belgic ruler of Camulodunum, and of Dubnovellaunus, his sub-king here, are found (**7**). Although Kent's opposition to Caesar meant that it did less well from trade with Rome than kingdoms north of the Thames, the local aristocracy bought Durovernon's brooches and cloth and Roman imports, while playing complex political games which were to lead refugee princelings to appeal for Roman aid on the death of Cunobelin, around AD 40.

3 *Later Neolithic bowl c. 3000–2500 BC. Found at Whitehall in the western suburbs, this vessel was handmade, round-based and decorated with finger-nail and finger-tip impressions. The reconstruction drawing shows a form and decoration typical of the period, in the Ebbsfleet style of the Peterborough tradition. The bowl and decorated cup c. 850–600 BC are reconstructed vessels of transitional late Bronze Age to early Iron Age period from Highstead near Chislet. They resemble fragments found at Castle Street in the ditch of a settlement enclosure.*

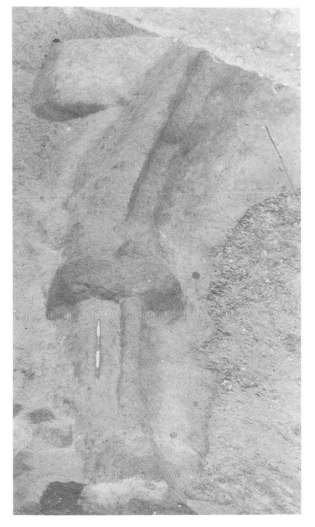

4 *The sophisticated triple-ditched enclosure with off-set entrances guarding the Belgic settlement first appeared in the 1940s. Rampart material and two phases of ditch, recut to 6m (19¹/₂ft) wide by 2m (6¹/₂ft) deep, were found near the Castle. Between AD 50 and 70 they were filled with rubbish and dismembered human bones.*

5 *These impressions preserved in the damp clay hint that a narrow-wheeled Belgic chariot drove along this Iron Age track through a herd of animals on their way to market in the first urban settlement.*

6 *Belgic and Roman pottery group: first to fourth centuries. On the left a native Belgic jar, a Rhineland flagon and samian cup span the Conquest period. Typical Canterbury products of the Flavian–Antonine period include the flagon, lid-seated jar and reed-flanged bowl. The later group of imported dark Upchurch, paler Gaulish and colour-coated Oxfordshire wares on the right includes rough handmade vessels showing later decline.*

7 *Coins of Cunobelin and Dubnovellaunus. Previously unknown, the ship coin of Cunobelin, supreme ruler in Camulodunum, is of bronze with a winged victory figure on the reverse. Dubnovellaunus, the Kentish ruler, is shown riding with a hunting weapon (with a lion on the reverse), on his copper coin. Both were probably in use during the Roman conquest.*

Topic: The Topography of the City

Canterbury's strong visual impact on travellers approaching from north, south and, particularly, west, which once made pilgrims drop to their knees at Golden Hill, appears in countless prints, particularly in the nineteenth century when Gothic romanticism was added to its charms. The topics attached to each chapter look in detail at particular aspects of city topography left by successive ages; this one traces the evolution of a compact and enduring image of a walled city, its red roofs grouped round its cathedral.

Belgic and Roman influence (8)

About AD 270 the Romans decided to exclude the earlier industrial suburb west of the river from the new wall circuit, but to include an old south-eastern cemetery area and one burial mound within it (see Topic: Chapter 2). This decision dictated the city's future image since the durable walls were not shifted by later rebuilding. The position of the city gates was related to the Roman road network in East Kent, surviving as today's 'A' roads, although, in the early Saxon period, the approaches from outside became blurred immediately beyond the walls. As the superimposed map (9) shows, the Roman street alignment was lost after the fifth century, but today's plan was partly determined by the crossroads in the decayed Roman theatre, a source of building stone into Norman times. When, in 1174, Henry II donned sackcloth at St Dunstan's Church for his penance at Becket's tomb, he hardly appreciated that church and churchyard lay within the right-angle turn created when the early trackway along the gravel terrace turned towards the fording place among the alder groves. Within this angle lay a large Roman cemetery beyond the Belgic suburb.

Saxon and medieval

Roman cemeteries, strung along the Richborough road outside the wall, may account for the location of St Martin's Church in this area, but certainly provided the site for St Augustine's first Abbey and burial church (see Topic: Chapter 3). His first Cathedral, on the higher ground in the north-east angle of the Roman city wall, later stimulated the evolution of Burgate, Sun Street and Palace Street along its other two boundaries. Markets developed along the route from the southern Worthgate to the Cathedral. Modern tourists approaching the Buttermarket along Mercery Lane tread this track.

Changes in the river level caused Roman London Gate and Watling Street to cease to be used and a new High Street to evolve from Westgate to a New-in-gate at its eastern end. The river's new branch through the city in Saxon times brought mills to the western end where poor people lived in damp conditions; this, in time, brought two friary precincts there also. William the Conqueror had consolidated the old burial mound within the walls for his first castle; enough remained to allow the eighteenth-century improver, James Simmons, to create the present ornamental mound and walks (67). The development of the northern suburb owed much to Lanfanc's charitable foundations there (see Topic: Chapter 4), beyond the kink his palace created at the Borough, inside Northgate. From there, development spread outside the eastern stretches of city wall in an arc of markets to the Wincheap suburb, while St Augustine's developed their own wide market-place in Longport.

We owe our greatest visual debt to the Middle Ages, which provided contrasts of scale. From the French Gothic of William of Sens to John Wastell's perpendicular tower, architects at the Cathedral set it, as was said in 1942,

8 **(following page)** *Roman city map. Apart from area excavations, knowledge has grown since 1975 from numerous small excavations. The largest gap in knowledge, shown by the comparative scarcity of sites, is in the waterlogged area where ephemeral artefacts of poorer people would survive better.*

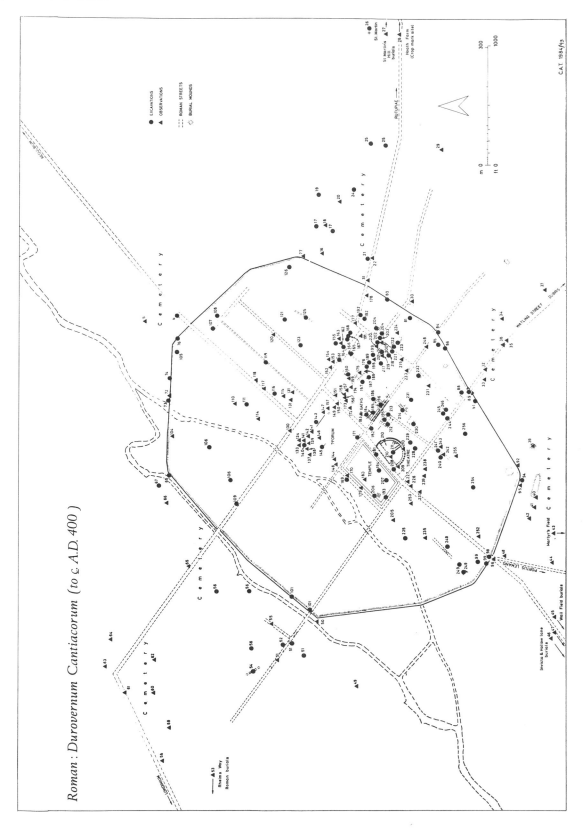

Roman : Durovernum Cantiacorum (to c. A.D. 400)

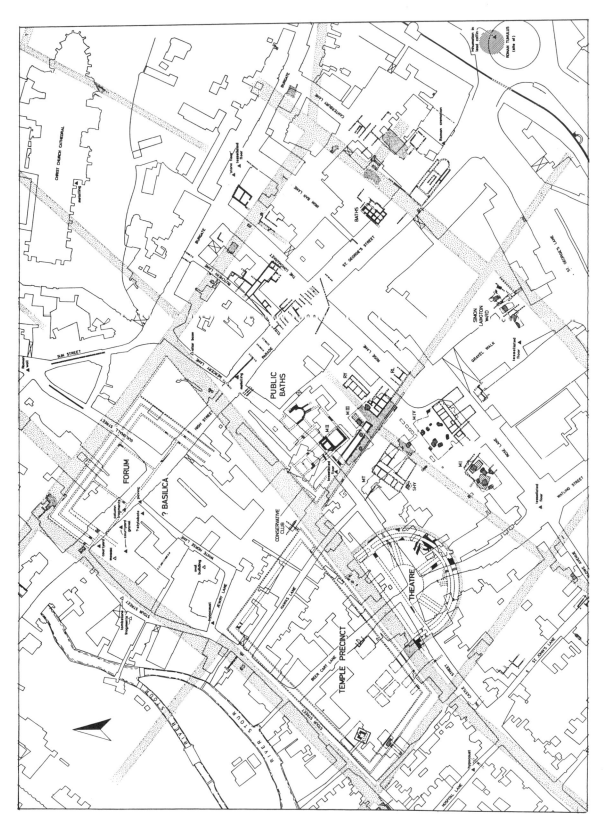

9 (preceding page) *Superimposed Roman street plan (updated in 1992). Durovernum's first street slants across the more regular grid of the 100s. The area of heaviest bombing in 1942 is that successively excavated since. Temple and baths were exposed in the 1980s redevelopments but Guildhall Street was cut and the Guildhall demolished before modern archaeology could reveal more than fragments of the forum.*

'like a jewel' in the city, while one of them, Henry Yevele, also provided its perfect foil in the magnificent Westgate. Pilgrims failing to enter the city before curfew, despite spurring their horses into a Canterbury pace, or canter, stayed in St Dunstan's Street which was lined with inns. Working for God or the King, architects did not plan these contrasts any more than they affected prosperous citizens building comfortable timber-framed houses or masterful priors providing spacious pilgrim inns (see Topics: Chapters 5 and 6). The topographical dominance of religious precincts and churches was overwhelming (**10**).

Destruction

The loss of monastic buildings in the sixteenth century, stretches of the city wall and Archbishops' Palace in the seventeenth century, city gates in the eighteenth century and much of the Georgian city in the Second World War may seem to record only decline. This was Daniel Defoe's perception in 1724: 'Its antiquity seems to be its greatest beauty. The houses are truly ancient and the many ruins of churches...and the smaller cells of religious people makes the place look like a general Ruin, a little recovered.' Celia Fiennes' and William Cobbett's middle-class eyes could see a thriving regional market town, its buildings 'handsome and neat' and 'remarkable for cleanliness and niceness notwithstanding it has a Cathedral in it'. The 1825 map (**11**) illustrates Canterbury's sources of wealth. Hop grounds and orchards encircle the city, while market gardens occupy the western friary precinct and

the refurbished Cattlemarket the eastern ditch. The new Dover turnpike created fashionable St George's Place whose residents could enjoy the lime walks and mound at Dane John. Most city gates and some buildings illustrated have gone but the new Military Road leads to the northern barrack blocks. Karl Marx, in 1866, felt that these barracks and a 'dismal, dry railway station' further marred an old and ugly town 'with no poetry about it'.

Victorian romanticism and after

Nevertheless, under his painting of St Augustine's Gate in 1833 (**12**) the popular local artist Sidney Cooper was moved to quote from *Hamlet*: 'To what base uses may we not return, Horatio? Why may not imagination trace the noble dust of Alexander till he find it stopping a bung hole?' When the painting was exhibited at the Royal Academy in 1886 St Augustine's site, no longer a brewery, had been transformed into an Anglican missionary college by the romantic revulsion of a young MP and this seat of ancient learning recovered. The Gothic revival architect, Butterfield, received the important commission to restore it. Although the precinct is now divided between English Heritage, the King's School and an Anglican Higher Education College, the old idea of Canterbury as a home of education brought another Gothic building, St Edmund's School, in the nineteenth century to St Thomas's hill where, in 1965, the University of Kent at Canterbury (U.K.C.) opened. Holford, its first architect, tied his college designs specifically to the view of Cathedral and city from the hill (see Topic: Chapter 7), a tension as effective when viewed from the city (**colour plate 12**).

10 *A topographical map of Canterbury in 1500. The relative depopulation of the Castle area after the Black Death is clear. Populous suburbs nevertheless developed, inhabited by incomers and others, earning by both town and country work. The archbishop's, monastic and friary precincts dominate the topography.*

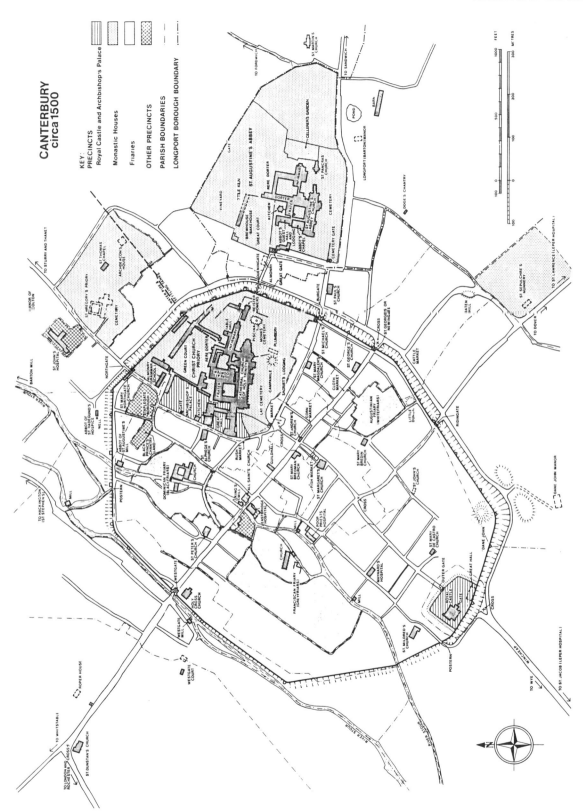

CANTERBURY circa 1500

KEY:
PRECINCTS
Royal Castle and Archbishop's Palace
Monastic Houses
Friaries
OTHER PRECINCTS
PARISH BOUNDARIES
LONGPORT BOROUGH BOUNDARY

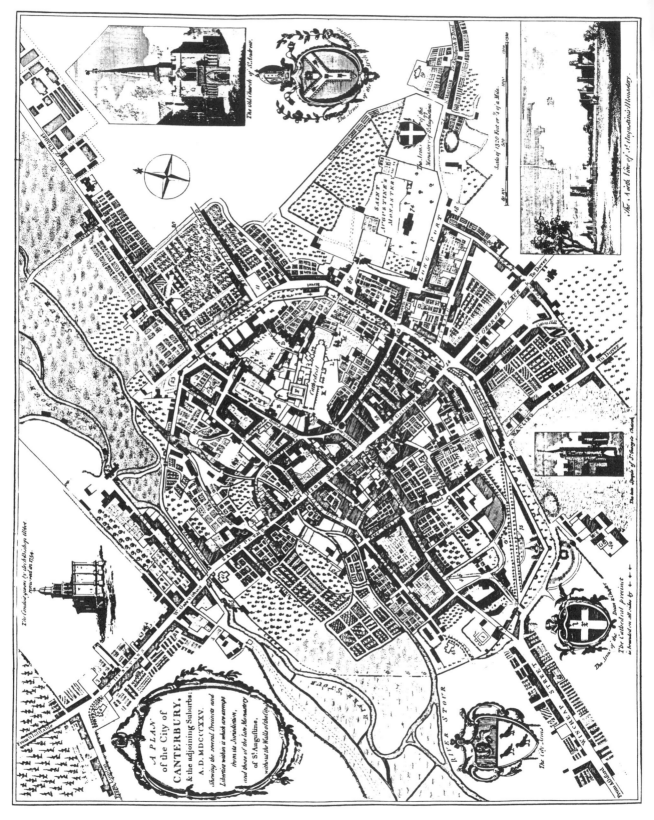

11 *A map of Canterbury in 1825. Appearing in* Gostling's Walks, *printed by James Simmons, this was a reissue of Doidge's map of 1788 with pictures added. It has not been updated to include the 1808 courthouse and prison beyond Longport.*

12 *St Augustine's Abbey Gate 1833 by Sidney Cooper. A typogravure by Bownsed and Valadon after the painting exhibited at the Royal Academy in 1886. When he sketched it from a cow-keeper's yard the premises were Beer and Bennett's Brewery and pleasure gardens.*

2
Durovernum Cantiacorum – a tribal capital

Durovernum's Roman history lasted as long as the period separating the present from Charles I's Canterbury honeymoon in 1625. While the last 369 years seem to us eventful, the Roman centuries often appear monotonously uniform, despite their sequence of conquest, rebellion, growth and decay. We know little about Canterbury's Roman beginnings and end, or about the size and lifestyle of its workforce; nothing of its local government and most about its material remains. These can be glimpsed among the pock-marks of wells and cesspits in a city continuously redeveloped during the fourteen following centuries. The unfolding story is illumined by area excavation in the city centre only since 1978 and by the random vignettes provided by rescue archaeology since the Second World War.

Early years
In AD 43 the invading army, crossing the Stour, soon left behind Durovernon, 'stronghold of the Cantiaci by the alder grove', to hunt its main adversary, the Catuvellauni, at Colchester. After early successes, showpiece towns grew quickly there and at London and Verulamium, to become objects of resentment and revenge during Boudica's revolt. Canterbury belongs, with Silchester, Chichester and Winchester, to a group of smaller towns where some development occurred before the rebellion. The other three lay among enemies of the Catuvellauni and grew with official encouragement, towards

the client-king Cogidubnus and towards the Atrebates at Silchester, whose ruler's appeal to Claudius had been the first pretext for invasion.

In Kent, where disruption was so short-lived, Rochester and Canterbury could grow into towns from Iron Age beginnings; other settlements, part-Romanized before the Conquest, developed differently and at varying rates. The defensive settlement at the Stour crossing, the hub of a new road wheel radiating to Richborough, Dover and London, presumably gave Durovernum Cantiacorum the edge over Rochester for promotion to *civitas* capital status. In return for status, its natural leaders took on obligations to the central government for the whole tribal area, not unlike the old British system of indirect rule in colonial Africa (**13**).

Although behind the battle-line, Durovernum may have had an early fort. Excavations at Canterbury Castle uncovered V-shaped ditches relating to a possible fortification built soon after the Conquest. It was briefly evacuated around 60; rebuilt when the early ditches were filled in with rampart material, skeletons and

13 *A map of Roman Kent. Nearer to Gaul than London, commanding the Stour gap and on the densely settled dip-slope, Durovernum was the natural capital. Roads and defences influenced settlement until villa estates colonized the Medway and Darenth valleys. Caesar distinguished West Kent's natives from East Kent's Belgae; later, Saxons colonized the West and Jutes the East. Thus Kent had two Roman towns and, from the seventh century, two sees.*

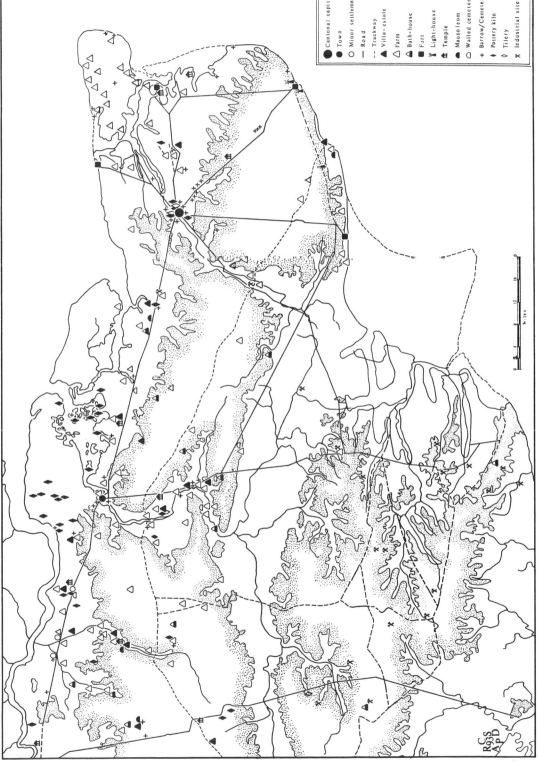

a pony carcase and finally abandoned 69–71 when troops were moved north.

One of several early roads leads from this point towards the centre, where changes were beginning in the 70s. Rectangular wooden buildings of Roman design, near which fine bronze horse-harness trappings and military belt-fittings have been found, stood among the round huts of the Belgic inhabitants. For them, life went on as before; they used their own coinage and local and imported pottery, burying these with their dead in areas within the later wall circuit.

Only around 100 were the unlucky occupants of central sites displaced, by dumping and levelling for the first big public buildings and the establishment of a more regular street grid. Some sites were to wait for twenty or thirty years for redevelopment.

The street grid

Durovernum Cantiacorum never had the regular chequerboard layout of other towns. On green-field sites at Silchester and Wroxeter, archaeologists have found deliberately-planned towns, encouraged by Nero and Hadrian. At Cirencester, two miles of walls, set with monumental gates, enclosed an area regularly planned from the centre outwards which never reached its ambitious limits.

Canterbury was fortunate in its Victorian engineer. James Pilbrow, FSA, trenching for main drainage, not only discovered the different orientation of Roman streets, but recorded, drew and photographed what he found, delivering a paper to the Antiquaries, published in 1871. It was left for S.S. Frere's pioneering digs between 1946 and 1960, in the wake of wartime bombing, to map the Roman city's plan. While his general orientation stands, recent excavations have considerably modified it. Three streets, so far, run roughly parallel, from the Dover and Richborough to the London sides of the city (that is south-east to north-west). Two others run at right angles to them. The street separating theatre from temple survived

in the new plan, but aslant and on the same alignment as two other early roads (see **9**). It seems that the evolving plan was modified when professional surveyors arrived and was fitted in where convenient. Other new roads served later infilling until major changes were caused by the late appearance of walls and gates in the 270s (see Topic). Every street discovered was made of rammed gravel, repeatedly repaired to considerable thickness and usually bordered by timber-lined or masonry drains, graded to soakaways. Durovernum emerged from the planner's hands with four central but irregularly shaped *insulae* containing theatre, temple, baths and forum/basilica. The *civitas* capital of the Cantiaci, the first a traveller from the settled lands would encounter in this new imperial out-post, was now to be suitably adorned with the trappings of civilized life (**14**).

Tacitus records that Agricola, the Governor from 79, encouraged privately-funded and civic building developments. Certainly Verulamium, Silchester and Cirencester went in for public display at this time. At Durovernum, the splendour of Corinthian capitals and marble detailing found on the temple site show that foreign craftsmen along with foreign materials were brought in for this purpose.

14 *A Roman* norma *from Watling Street. This rare bronze mitre-square, inscribed with its owner's name, came from the construction levels of a fourth-century house, replacing a masonry predecessor two hundred years older; both had tessellated floors.*

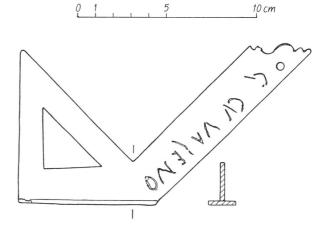

Canterbury's redevelopment problems since 1945 have luckily left chunks of this central core available for full-time excavation since 1978, although the forum/basilica area is still covered by large buildings, currently in use.

The theatre (see 9)

Roman Britain has, so far, revealed amphitheatres on the edges of towns but few theatres: there are those at Colchester and Canterbury of classical form, Verulamium's round theatre and an inscription relating to one at Brough-on-Humber. Perhaps our ancestors, too, were keener on sport than culture. The theatres, as at Canterbury, are close to temple sites, so resembling both Celtic sites in Roman Gaul and a classical tradition going back to Athens. In Rome's Celtic provinces, theatres seem to have done double duty as places for mass gatherings at native and Roman religious festivals and for entertainment. In early days, spectacles were probably sporting as often as dramatic.

Frere's 1950s' excavations first identified massive masonry, located by Pilbrow, as two successive theatres. Lying athwart built-up crossroads, remains are sighted frequently, but in fragments. Thanks to Pilbrow's meticulous recording, the archaeologists today can correlate findings, often only surviving as Norman robber trenches, to recreate these two theatres.

By 90, alongside the slanting road retained by the surveyors, an elliptical theatre probably already stood. A bank of earth and gravel carried tiered wooden seating, revetted by front and rear walls of tile-bonded flint. In the early third century, this amenity was replaced by a monumental classical theatre in conventional D-shape. It was built partly on massive vaulted masonry, covering the paved *cavea* 2.7m (9ft) wide, between its retaining walls. This gave access to banked seating facing the stage and orchestra. Findings recovered across an area measuring 71m (233ft) by nearly 60m (196ft), and the size of surviving foundations indicate a building dominating the city then as the

Cathedral does now. Always too large for any but occasional use, it influenced the topography of Canterbury's later streets and was a source of building material. Even Lanfranc's Norman crypt at the Cathedral contains reused Roman masonry.

The temple (colour plate 1)

Across the street from the theatre lay a large precinct surrounded by masonry walls on four sides; a colonnaded portico, 3m (10ft) wide, lined it. Contemporary with the first theatre and baths, it had a long life. The courtyard was resurfaced up to six times over two centuries. Disrepair and robbing littered the fourth-century surface with over one thousand pieces of imported marble fragments. Mouldings, veneers, Corinthian capitals and a large fluted column shaft must indicate a classical temple, since these do not normally decorate Celtic shrines. A lined fountain basin was placed on the central theatre axis but no temple has yet appeared. In the corner, built at the same time, stood a rectangular wooden Celtic shrine, composed of a clay-floored inner cell and outer ambulatory. Other shrines may have stood here too, since public worship on civic occasions concentrated on processions to make offerings at open-air altars. Courtyards had to be large enough for such ceremonies, but shrines to shelter protective gods and receive votive gifts could be small. The earlier surfaces reveal little dropped by worshippers, but once colonnade and shrine were demolished in the fourth century, possibly for a market-place, the whole area is littered with late pottery and small coins.

Other public buildings

For over 200 years Durovernum was to enjoy social and sports centres which the modern city still lacks on the same scale. The *insula* north of the theatre was simultaneously developed as a public baths complex. Since the main block lies askew in its gravelled *palaestra* or exercise yard, it may also have started ahead of the new street grid, but was in use by the 120s. Along the edge of two new shopping streets, a porticoed colonnade bordered the yard. A wall to the east fronted a narrow lane beyond which a wealthy grandee equipped his own house with a seven-room private bath-suite.

The public baths were often altered. A second-century refit turned the early cold plunge bath into a heated room, and major changes coincided with the huge new theatre building in the third century, when Durovernum obviously prospered. A bather would then enter the *apodyterium* (changing area) through a western portico, paved with *tesserae*, after which *frigidaria* (cold rooms) connected with a stone-paved plunge bath. The tepid rooms lie unexcavated but hot baths and a magnificent apsidal-ended *caldarium* (hot steam room) have been found with external *praefurnia* (stoke holes) and drains. The *caldarium* may have lasted throughout the building's life, with occasional repair. By the 350s the baths had fallen out of use. Curved box-flues for removing hot gases through arched roofs lay on the collapsed *pilae* stacks of the underfloor heating system (**15**).

15 *A Roman bath house, St Margaret's Street. This unusual spacer held the two walls of the hot room apart for hot air to circulate. A flue-tile has been reused to support the floor. The curved flue tiles arched over the roof allowing the air finally to escape. Found in a shop cellar, they lay on collapsed* pilae *stacks, covered by fallen wall plaster.*

Another free-standing, later bath-house was found after the Second World War below Woolworths. Possibly built as a commercial venture, around 220, it was substantially altered about 355. The number of heated rooms was then reduced, but new entertainments were provided. For example, over two hundred late coins were found in what may have been a gaming room. It was badly damaged by fire soon afterwards and from 360 became ruinous (see **73**).

Only random traces of the forum and basilica exist. Large expanses of courtyard gravel, a stone-paved portico and blocks of masonry lie below the County Hotel, Museum environs and in cellars below the High Street.

A *mansio*?

Canterbury's position, a horse ride from the coast, has always made it a city of inns. An empire held together by efficient communications must have planned a *mansio* or inn for Durovernum, where messengers and officials could rest and change horses. Two candidates have surfaced recently. A second-century buttressed flint building, inside the London Gate, beside Watling Street, contained small rooms round a central hall, decorated with painted plaster. Only the north-east third of this building could be excavated. Silchester's *mansio* is similarly placed, but includes a lavish bath-house courtyard. In 1991 excavations at Longmarket extended our knowledge of a mosaic-floored property, found after the Second World War and now the site of Canterbury's Roman Museum. In the mid-second century, a wide corridor was built to link it to a new bath-house, erected in the courtyard of an earlier house. A full suite of changing, cold, tepid and hot rooms, with hot plunge bath and *laconica* (sauna) went up, later altered for economy, by the separate heating of some rooms. By the fourth century it had gone out of use. There is not enough evidence to identify either building positively as our missing *mansio*.

Houses, shops and workshops

The words 'civilization' and 'citizenship' tell us how central towns (*civitates*) were to Roman thinking. In Iron Age Britain, settlements like Durovernum were recent and impermanent, and had neither local government nor symbolic functions. Once Durovernum was designated the administrative centre of the Cantiaci, buildings reflected both downwards and upwards expectations. The public buildings described, so unlike native huts, created a feeling of belonging to a greater whole, as did language, coinage and emperor worship. The houses, shops, workshops and minor temples reflected peoples' new aspirations. Once the old warrior leaders became the new civic heads and acquired town houses, luxury trades to supply them grew up. Importers brought in a wide variety of continental goods. A building boom established tile and lime kilns, chalk and gravel quarries and builders' workshops. The Belgic potters, weavers and metalworkers continued to improve their own skills from handling imports.

Native gods were worshipped alongside the Roman pantheon. Three other possible temples, dating from the late second century, are known. One lies below St Gabriel's Chapel at the Cathedral. It had two or three rooms with tesselated floors, one containing a mosaic. Votive figurines representing Silenus and a rough native deity lay on the surface (**16**). A courtyard for religious use appears from recent excavation to have been situated near St George's Church, where a horse statuette was found (**17**). An earlier horse find in Burgate may also suggest the worship of the Celtic Epona. The German goddess Nehallenia and pipeclay figurines of mother goddesses, probably from family shrines, were studied by Dr Frank Jenkins, the watchdog of Canterbury archaeology in the 1950s and 1960s. Apart from the Butchery Lane house, found after the War, a small sample of 28 private houses on the Marlowe site and other incomplete city centre properties have been examined. Private town houses were built from the early 100s, many continuing for

16 *Votive figurine from St Gabriel's Chapel (Cathedral). This figure, in hooded Gaulish cloak, lay with other ex-voto objects, including a bull's horn and a bronze Silenus, on the coloured tessellated floor of a probable three-room Roman temple, disused after 300. He was once coated in mica-gilt, as at second-century Trier, where the healing temple of Mars Lenus contained dwarf figures from Aesculapian cults. (6cm by 3cm (2$\frac{1}{2}$in by 1$\frac{1}{4}$in.))*

17 *A pipeclay horse figure. Made in Central Gaul and dated to the second century, this white pipeclay figure is the second horse found in Canterbury. It is 12.4cm (5in) long and was probably a votive offering, perhaps to Mars-Epona.*

several centuries with alterations and additions. The first were of timber; later, timber on masonry foundations or entirely masonry construction was favoured for the popular winged-corridor houses. Building density on *insulae* grew throughout the second and early third centuries and existing houses were modernized by adding central heating, tessellated and mosaic floors and painted plaster or marble veneered walls; several incorporated a private bath-suite. Canterbury's wealthy have always preferred the higher ground where these finds cluster. How overcrowded shopkeepers' families were, how many servants lived in, or how developed the waterlogged western sector of the city was, remain mysteries. Bakers' shops and a possible enameller's workshop have been found and museum artefacts show that craftsmen included silversmiths and makers of metal jugs, lamps, keys, bells and steelyards, bronze furniture fittings, and bone counters, spoons and pins. Among imports were gold and silver jewellery, jet hair-pins, samian tableware and glass, together with luxury foods and oils and German and Mediterranean wines; Whitstable oysters were commonplace.

A sizeable industrial suburb existed on the London side of the Stour. In its regular network

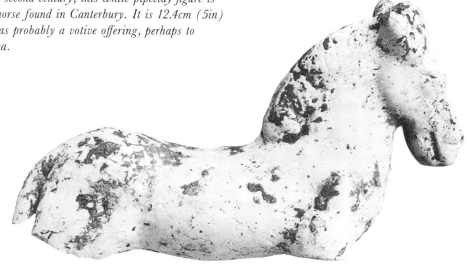

of lanes lived metalworkers, potters and tile-makers. Originally part of the growing city, the decision to leave it outside the wall circuit in 270 condemned this suburb to wither in the next century.

Pottery (see 6)

The Conquest boosted the existing import trade in samian and other fine Gaulish pottery, in both range and quantity, which was supplemented by grey fine-ware from north-west Kent. The native industry flourished, too, for the first 150 years, when sandy coarse-ware, made in Durovernum by local and possibly Gaulish immigrant potters, was sold all over the *civitas* region in East Kent. Little of it travelled far, however, either cross-channel or to London. Perhaps originally made for the military establishment at Richborough, it was soon available in new forms, colours and decorations. The new manufacture of flagons shows how wine-drinking caught on. Between 90 and 130 our first named inhabitants, Juvenalis and Valentinus, were stamping their *mortaria* and *amphorae* of imported white gault clays. The local industry suffered from the late 100s onwards. First black-burnished ware from the Thames estuary and then, early in the 200s, colour-coated Oxfordshire and Nene valley ware, brought round by boat, broke into Durovernum's market. They replaced Gaulish and Rhenish imports to dominate the local scene until about 375. Old fashioned local coarse-ware products went downmarket and, when a coin-based economy vanished in the fifth century, only a limited range of crude hand-made vessels survived.

Cemeteries

Durovernum continued to cremate its dead, as before, until the third century, when interment gradually became general. A change in fashion, as in the opposite direction today, was under way, irrespective of the spread of Christianity. Even after 313 when Christianity was officially tolerated, grave goods could still adorn a corpse or offer it respect and graves were not always orientated west to east.

Romans excluded burials from within cities, yet the dead were not to be lonely nor neglected, so cemeteries grew along major roads. On the Reculver, Richborough, Dover and Lympne roads such early cemeteries exist. The largest yet found lies between the two roads towards London; the modern London Road still skirts the cemetery's western edge before turning towards the Westgate; it was used from the early 100s onwards. Cremations in adapted cooking pots and *amphorae* are accompanied by food and wine dishes, coins and lamps to aid and illumine the departed on their last journey.

The line of later defences cuts across earlier burial places, and several burial mounds, none excavated, of late first- or early second-century date, were so separated. Two disappeared below the 1860s' railway station; one truncated hillock displays used cars but the fourth, within the walls, became the first Norman castle and later the focus of an eighteenth-century park. Later inhumation cemeteries lie outside but near the walls. In the 200s, two auxiliary soldiers met an unexplained end. Below the floor of a possible tavern they were stuffed into a cramped and shallow grave; their cavalry *spathae* were thrown in after them. The museum houses the restored swords where you may speculate on our first possible murder mystery (**18**).

Last days

The city known to Roman travellers as Durovernum Cantiacorum, in the Antonine Itinerary of 220, still kept its name in the seventh-century Ravenna Cosmography. We can trace this period with some confidence, through gradual decay, into the 450s. Thereafter, daylight breaks in again only after St Augustine's arrival in 597.

In the late third century, although old landmarks began to decay, new buildings went up, others were refurbished and the city walls were constructed. The temple portico was demol-

18a *Double burial (Heritage Museum). A small, hastily-dug grave appeared under the floor of a wooden house built on a cemetery, abandoned after 270. One man was thrown in, his legs twisted to fit; another lay top to toe over him. Their cavalry* spathae *were thrown in after them, one still bearing part of its wooden scabbard and bronze chape. Hob-nails and bronze belt-studs survived.*

b *Reconstruction of the double burial. Cavalry auxiliaries wore long double-edged slashing swords, unlike the legionary's* gladius. *The bronze horse trappings come from an earlier city centre find. How the men died is a mystery.*

ished, a new courtyard was laid and maybe a market took over; the latest small coins are dated 380–90 but were current for much longer. Cobblers and bone-workers set up in the baths' *palaestra*, while the baths themselves and the possible *mansio* were crumbling. The bathhouse drain overflowed, silting up the old lane. Wooden lean-to shops were then built against the *palaestra* wall. Other new buildings also encroached on old streets into the fifth century. In some places, ruined second-century houses were recolonized by timber buildings or industrial workshops within their walls. The south gate of the Riding Gate was shut for the last time, and its vaulted carriageway became a smith's workshop (**colour plate 3**).

The late Christian community vexes historians. How many it numbered and whether worship was mainly in house-churches or took place on special occasions to honour the dead or to remember holy people is unknown, but evidence can point in all three directions. A silver hoard buried outside the London Gate in about 410 reveals the silversmith's insecurity at the time. The clientele were still wealthy enough to buy silver spoons and included Christians commissioning a spoon and *ligula*, with Chi-Rho monograms, perhaps for use at home (**19**). Although excavation has failed to find either a house of which St Martin's could be the chapel, or a graveyard, of which it could be the mausoleum, its chancel core seems to be of Roman rather than seventh-century construction. Professor Brooks argues for a possible cemetery-chapel origin for the later churches of St Dunstan, St Sepulchre and St Paul

19 *A silver hoard of c. 410 (Heritage Museum). This hoard, reassembled by chance, was adjudged treasure trove, since the silversmith never reclaimed it from beside the London Gate. The pointed* ligula *(12.9cm (5in) long) and a spoon bear Chi-Rho monograms to attest to Roman Christianity here. There were ten other spoons, gold and silver jewellery and eight coins (not shown), the latest of Honorius (393–423). Two silver ingots, each weighing a Roman pound, were probably Imperial accession gifts.*

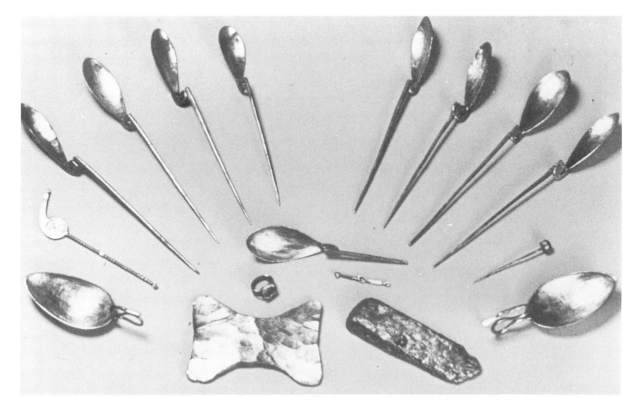

and points to the tenacious memory into St Augustine's day that St Martin's and the Cathedral site were once Roman churches.

Four early pagan burials, following local cremation and inhumation customs, have appeared in Roman cemeteries which obviously remained in use into the 'Dark Ages'. Yet one remarkable early fifth-century burial did break old taboos and was found within the temple precinct (**20**). A family was carefully interred, sitting under a roof, the woman with one girl in her arms and another at her feet; the man with the old family dog on his lap – it had worn-down teeth and a healed fracture. While Roman keys, chains and bangles adorned the females, their imported glass beads give us this late date. How they derived their wealth, and what their burial tells of urban decay and possible epidemics are enigmas. The relative scarcity of villas in East Kent indicates that Durovernum may have been the secure base from which wealthier landowners ran their estates. A scattered goldsmith's hoard, overly-

20 *A fifth-century burial. The straw- or grass-lined burial pit within the Roman temple precinct had several notable features. The restored bangles are Roman bronze; others were of silver, bone and ivory, but the Germanic beads of glass and amber seem to be imports. One child probably died from a blow to the head, the others perhaps in an epidemic.*

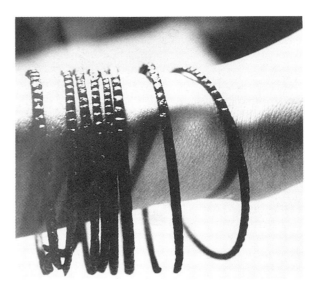

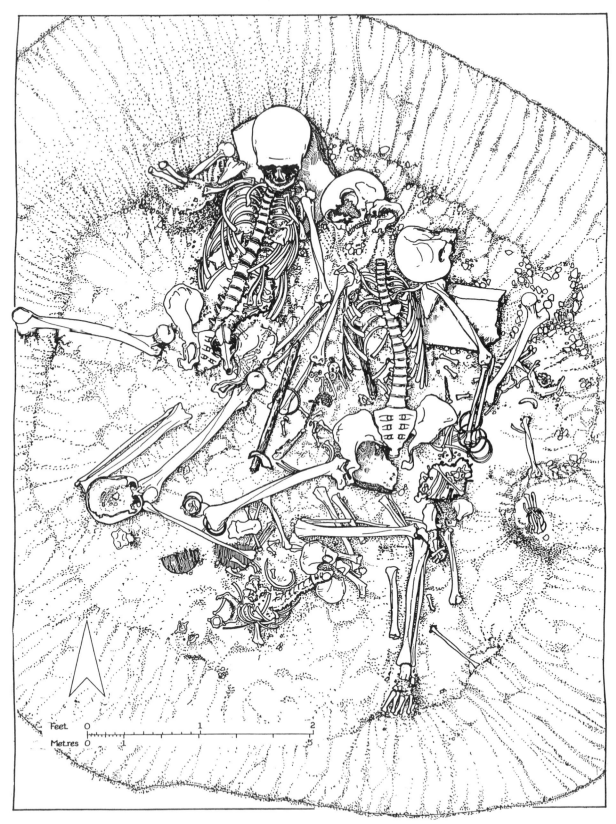

Feet 0   1   2

Metres 0   1   5

ing a late Roman courtyard, contained a South Gaulish Visigothic *tremiss* of *c*. 480, not used as currency but clipped for melting. For whom was he making jewellery at this date?

Decay gradually overtook most of the city, for dark-earth deposits of varying depth seal most excavated Roman buildings. Similarly, some 'transitional' pottery, although a small sample, may link the last Roman to the first Germanic examples which arrive around 450. These were handmade and not fired in a kiln. Forty Jutish-type huts have now been found. Current theory favours several waves of continental refugees, from the late fifth century onwards, arriving to coexist, then to intermarry with the locals. Having left behind marauding war-bands and encroaching floods, they doubtless felt lucky to be squatters among the ruins. Certainly, organized urban life had ended.

Topic: Roman Walls and Gates (21)

Canterbury's defences are Rome's most enduring and constraining legacy. Somner, in 1640, correctly related East Kent's road system to Canterbury and identified stretches of Roman wall and three gates; only research after the Second World War allows the following positive statements to be made:

*When the defensive bank and wall were being built in 270–90, no earlier bank stood on the line which encloses 52.6ha (130 acres).

*Except on the western river frontage, a ditch about 18m (59ft) wide by 5m (16$\frac{1}{2}$ft) deep provided soil for the gravel-capped bank. This tailed back behind the wall for at least 6 to 9m (20 to 29$\frac{1}{2}$ft). The ditch lay in front of a cobbled berm extending 3m (10ft) from the wall face (**colour plate 2**).

*The wall, built of mortared coursed flint, sandstone boulders and reused stone had no bonding courses. It remains up to 3.5m (11$\frac{1}{2}$ft) high, embedded in the reconstructed medieval defences and an amazing 6m (20ft) high in the wall of St Mary Northgate Church (**22**).

*One internal and two possible external towers have been found but we do not know if any projected before or behind its wall site.

*Five gates have been part-excavated or surveyed (**23**). Two more almost certainly existed. Only Ridingate and Burgate are thought to have been dual-carriageway and none were monumental.

London Gate Excavations in the 1950s first proved the date of the walls; also that they extended to the river and were contemporary with the bank. The single arch had neither guard-chamber nor flanking towers since the earlier gravelled roadway of Watling Street ran through a flint-revetted tunnel in the 3.3m (11ft) wide bank. To the south-west, outside in the berm, the silver hoard (**19**) was hidden about 410.

West and North Gates London Gate could hardly rank as the main entrance from the capital. The west-bank Belgic suburb and an internal street traced westwards from Burgate determine the probable site of a substantial west gate where the wall takes a dog-leg, as at Worthgate and Ridingate. Saxon churches are recorded above Westgate and Northgate, where a third-century gate must have spanned the earlier Reculver road. Indeed, St Mary Northgate's chancel remained above the gate until its demolition in 1830.

Burgate Recent excavation found the mid-first-century road to Richborough, so often remetalled that it provided a solid base for the gate of the 270s. Only a greensand block from its southern side survived the fifteenth-century rebuild of what was probably a Roman dual-carriageway gate which became the main entry to the Saxon inner burh.

Before the 270s Durovernum needed no defence, but the end of the third century was insecure. Governments answered barbarian pressure on frontiers by increasing the forces attached to the Channel fleet. This in turn prompted the attempted coup by Carausius and Allectus. Rebuilding work at the 'Saxon

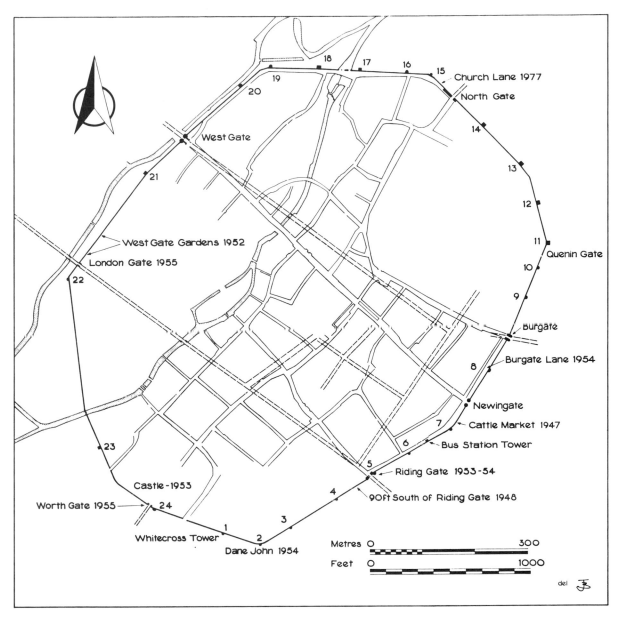

Metres 0 ——————————————— 300

Feet 0 ——————————————— 1000

del JS

Shore' forts of Reculver, Richborough, Dover and Lympne is all dated to around 270–290; Durovernum's strategic position, where the roads from the forts meet to cross the Stour, accords with a similar date for the defences there. A command post may have been based here, as recent finds of military belt fittings in late Roman levels suggest.

It was sensible to utilize the Stour's natural defence, but this decision abandoned half the

21 *Roman gates and walls.*

original Iron Age township. The southern quarter may have been included in compensation, although few streets have been traced. One consequence of the new wall circuit was the decline of the east–west street dividing the central *insulae* which now had no outlet (**24**). Streets in the northern quarter suffered the same fate.

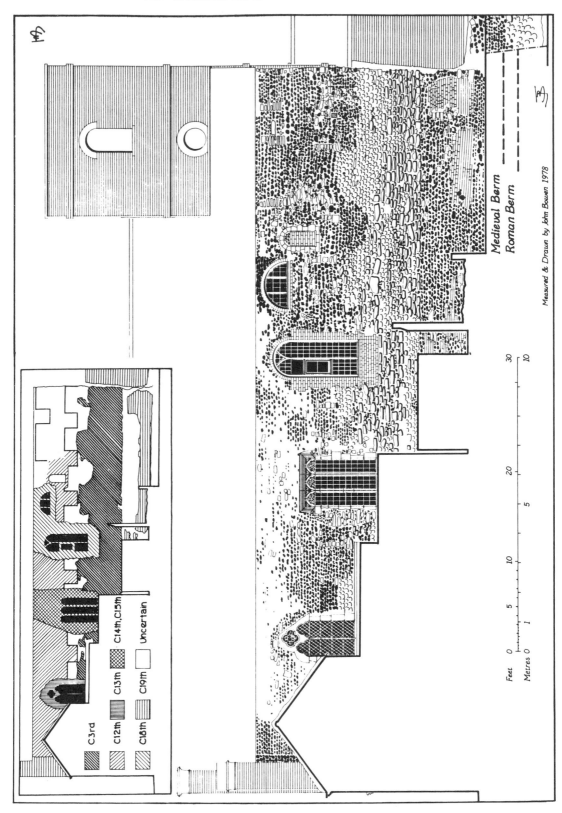

Medieval Berm

Roman Berm

Measured & Drawn by John Bowen 1978

C3rd
C12th
C13th
C14th, C15th
C16th
C19m
Uncertain

22 *St Mary Northgate wall. While the chancel remained above the Northgate, the medieval church expanded westwards as the extramural suburb grew, to incorporate in its north wall a standing section of Roman wall. It stands to 6m (20ft), not counting its crenellated parapet, possibly repaired with Norman Caen-stone merlons. It is now visible from a small public garden.*

23 *Worthgate. This gate, drawn by Stukeley in 1722, survived until 1791 and had a single arch, set at a dog-leg in the wall circuit. A road led through it to Portus Lemanis. It appears to have had internal guard-chambers.*

Worth Gate (a Roman Work) Canterbury
6, oct 1722,

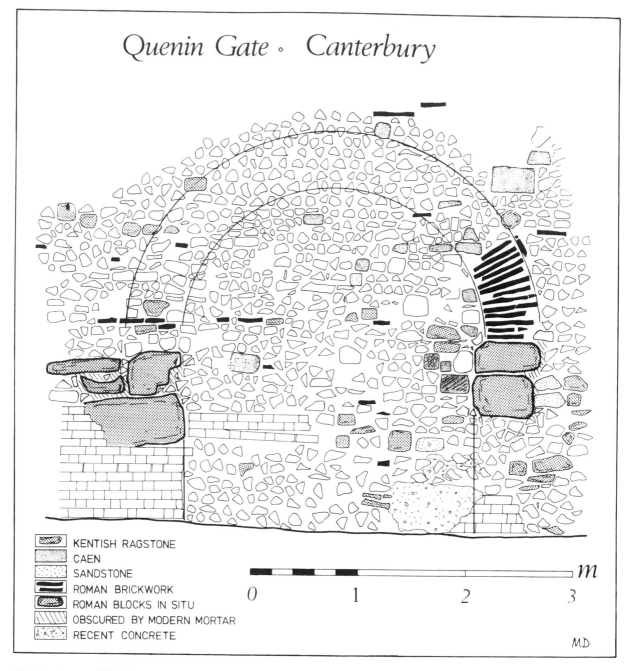

Quenin Gate · Canterbury

KENTISH RAGSTONE
CAEN
SANDSTONE
ROMAN BRICKWORK
ROMAN BLOCKS IN SITU
OBSCURED BY MODERN MORTAR
RECENT CONCRETE

0   1   2   3   *m*

MD

24 *Queningate. This Roman gate was the short cut to the Richborough road. It is visible in the Broad Street car-park, embedded in the city wall. Greensand ashlars support part of a brick arch spanning 2.6m (6ft).*

3

Cantwaraburh – the Christian revival

Durovernum, by and large, was typical of other Roman tribal capitals; Cantwaraburh, in its early revival, its unique religious status and the great men it therefore attracted, was very different from most Saxon towns. The city was strong enough to bounce back after Viking devastation, to assume by 1066 its recognizable modern topographical form and regional role.

In the darkness of the sub-Roman period came a mongrel war-band from the low-lying area between Jutland and Frisia. The story of how Hengist, the mercenary leader, displaced Vortigern, the Kentish 'tyrant', is a unique survival. Recent textual criticism, combined with archaeology, indicates that East Kent was soon transformed, more by negotiation and the infiltration of further boat-people in the wake of the warriors, than by bloody and protracted take-over. Some evidence of coexistence and continuity of occupation is emerging along Watling Street, which traverses the easily farmed dip-slope of the North Downs, and on villa-estates, as well as in the cemeteries and city centre of Durovernum. Certainly Kent was uniquely fortunate in how early it acquired a settled order and a royal dynasty. By 500, continental trade links were reopened, as the rich grave goods from royal cemeteries at Bifrons and Eastry reveal. However, itinerant kings, ruling from scattered *Villae Regales*, had no need of an up-river walled town, preferring the Wantsum customs post at Sarre. Not only did Durovernum's street grid disappear, but

Roman roads into the city fell into disuse; only at the gates do Roman and medieval streets overlap and no early cemeteries lie outside.

St Augustine's mission

Kent's monopoly of trade with the Franks enabled its king, Ethelbert, to be acknowledged as 'Bretwalda', or overlord, by other Saxon kings south of the Humber and secured his marriage to the Frankish Christian princess, Bertha. Pope Gregory therefore naturally targeted Kent for his missionary venture in 597, enlisting Frankish aid to stiffen Augustine's flagging resolve. To 40 obedient Romans, from Gregory's own St Andrew's monastery, it was inconceivable to site a see anywhere other than in a Roman town. Bede wrote that after Ethelbert's baptism, he gave Augustine a supposedly Roman building to 'recover' as the first Cathedral. Whatever had survived above ground, discoveries at the Cathedral in 1993 suggest that Augustine built anew. Narrow foundations of reused Roman rubble, supporting mortared Roman brick walls, lay below the nave's east end. With its western narthex and northern *porticus* the building closely resembled the early churches at St Augustine's Abbey (see **35**). Its base cut into dark earth containing pottery of *c.* 450–550, which in turn sealed a Roman street lined with buildings, one of which was found in 1973 south of the nave. The modern nave altar may stand over the core of the first missionary Cathedral. In the interim, the monks had used an extramural Roman building, restored by Queen Bertha and dedicated to St Martin. The monks needed an establishment separate from the archbishop's household of priests and acolytes, so the king granted part of an extramural Roman inhumation cemetery to become a monastic precinct, containing the royal and archiepiscopal burial church and the chapel of St Pancras (for all these sites see Topic).

In the missionary period it seems possible that, as at basilicas in Rome, monks and the archbishop's household joined for the three principal services, while the monks saw to the rest of the daily liturgy, setting the priests among them free to found and recover their churches, preach and baptize. Later missions to Northumbria sent back to Canterbury for cantors to teach singing 'in the Roman fashion'. Even if the much later extramural parish churches of St Paul, St Dunstan and St Sepulchre, located on or near Romano-British cemeteries, began as Roman cemetery chapels, it is unlikely that they were the only other Christian buildings in seventh-century Canterbury. Thanks to the lingering tradition that any brick or stone building had once been a church, some may even have been restarted in Roman secular buildings, such as those near St George's Church, glimpsed in 1947–9 and 1992. Bede, telling how Archbishop Mellitus quenched a city centre fire, mentions the church of the Four Crowned Martyrs, saints whose basilican shrine lay close to the pope's own monastery. Some of their relics may have arrived in 601, with reinforcements from Rome, when Gregory also sent relics of Pope Sixtus to augment the validity of a local Sixtus, whose cult had apparently survived.

A new topography

Augustine must have found a population to convert within the walls, but the founding of the see undoubtedly provided the stimulus for renewal. The Roman city walls and surviving buildings defined where development occurred. City-centre excavations have located over 30 mainly sunken huts of seventh-century and later date (**25**). Some cut through disused Roman streets and buildings long gone, but others respected Roman alignments and must have used the protection and material of standing walls. The huts were often recut and lay clustered in the old centre round the ruined theatre; the modern crossroads at its heart shows how Roman Watling Street got lost in the process. Loom-weights and spindle-whorls, pottery and leather reveal the life of a reviving market on a new axis from Roman Worthgate towards, not Northgate, but the Cathedral (**26**). Pottery finds show that wares from Ipswich and northern France were arriving in the years after St Augustine, and by 630 gold coins were being struck at the Canterbury mint. In 1982 evidence of life and death emerged when the reoccupation, around 600, of a Roman cremation cemetery was found in London Road. Besides glass handleless palm cups, reused Roman vessels and a 'sceatta' coin, a remarkable inlaid gold filigree pendant, with a central cross, revealed how a Kentish goldsmith reapplied his marvellous skill for a Christian customer (see back cover). Nevertheless, evidence from north and south of the centre suggests that much of the city was either still unoccupied or used for farming.

Today's Cathedral precinct possibly also began to take shape. Ethelbert probably located his royal hall on high, dry ground near the Cathedral church, already defended on two

25 *Reconstruction of a Saxon hut.* Grubenhaüser *or sunken huts, like examples from the German homelands, were found in groups across central Canterbury. Dating from the seventh-century revival, they contained evidence of weaving, potting and leather making.*

26 *Loom-weights found in a sunken hut. These clay weights for tautening warp threads on upright looms were found in a sunken hut and are about seventh-century in date. They reveal the town's revival in the wake of St Augustine.*

sides by the Roman walls. Professor Brooks suggests that the line of modern Burgate and the Borough whose names reveal the 'stronghold' element of the Old English, perpetuates the inner 'burh' of the Cant-ware, which was possibly defended by bank or palisade.

Canterbury's influence

In 669, an elderly Levantine polymath of superb organizational skill became archbishop. Between his sixty-seventh and eightieth years, Theodore of Tarsus transformed Canterbury, archbishopric and English Church, as dramatically as Lanfranc of Pavia, a later sexagenarian. Despite enduring links with the Papacy, through the persons of the first five archbishops, Canterbury had been sidetracked. Pope Gregory expected that Augustine, with Ethelbert's backing, would found a permanent see in London; its reversion to paganism in the next reign left Canterbury, almost by accident, with the primacy in name only. Wessex and East Anglia were converted from the Continent and the Celtic missionaries from Iona and Lindisfarne had largely evangelized Northumbria. In 664, the crucial Synod of Whitby had opted to remain under Rome without formal representation from Canterbury. Touring the country, charming key men like St Cuthbert, forming dioceses, holding Synods which pronounced on faith and practice, Theodore gave unity, order and discipline to the post-missionary church and reasserted Canterbury's spiritual supremacy with the Saxon kingdoms which Kentish kings had lost in secular terms.

As importantly, he and his friend Abbot Hadrian founded at Canterbury a school of international repute, attracting scholars from Europe and Ireland. A product of the Schools of Antioch and Constantinople, fluent in four biblical languages, Theodore, like some Schweitzer in Lambaréné, expounded the scripture in basic form to men ignorant of other languages or the Mediterranean world. His pupils ensured his continuing influence; Aldhelm's writing was to permeate Saxon monastic teaching; he describes Theodore, 'like a wild boar, beset by Irish hounds, using the sharpened tooth of his logic' against his students' arguments. Through Albinus, next abbot at Canterbury, Bede verified material for his History, and through Benedict Biscop learning spread, via Jarrow and the School of York, to Alcuin and thereby to the court of Charlemagne. Besides scholars, produce poured into Canterbury from land grants to Archbishopric and Abbey begun by Ethelbert. Thirty-six out of 89 Domesday manors were acquired in this early period.

The eighth to the tenth centuries

Before 700 the Stour ports of Fordwich and Sandwich appear in documents. Despite the overlordship, first of Mercia, then of Wessex, they enabled Canterbury to prosper, rather as Hamwic benefited Winchester. Wessex royal princes were under-kings in Kent, a port-reeve organized markets and tolls and Canterbury had borough status from 814. The river affected topography by developing a second branch through the city to create the island of Binnewith between it and the Westgate, an unhealthy area frequently flooded. The street connecting Westgate to the eastern gap in the walls, later filled by Newingate, became dominant, as it has remained. Halfway up, where it widened into a market-place, a middle row, which included a church, later developed. Another middle row possibly existed on the old axial road from Worthgate to the Cathedral. Fairly regular lanes grew from these two streets lined by properties with long plots at the rear. Unfortunately, houses on wooden cills leave few traces; those excavated may be secondary buildings surviving when frontage properties were rebuilt. A by-law prescribing a two-foot eaves drip between houses shows how the town filled up, although the southern quarter remained agricultural, with records describing 6–20 acre (2.4–8 ha) plots let as orchard, pasture and arable.

Plentiful everyday pottery and small finds

from bone combs to loom-weights hardly match the documentary evidence of prosperity (**27**). From 766 Canterbury officially minted Offa's silver pennies and by 930 it had seven mints to London's eight, four being royal, two archiepiscopal and one belonging to St Augustine's (**28**). Forums are mentioned inside and outside the walls and England's first recorded gild. A charter of *c.* 860 mentions a gild of *cnihtas*, or agents, retained by neighbouring magnates to manage their city warehouses and cattle pens; by 1066 they had become the burgess gild. As well as fraternities of inner-city and suburban inhabitants, an artisans' organization existed for the many *gemettan*, identified as living-in labourers entitled to meals. Named streets like Wistraet and Burgate appear and excavation has revealed streets cutting into Roman ramparts at Worthgate, Northgate and near Queningate. The Cathedral precinct was enlarged southwards by a lay cemetery opening on to Burgate. Recent excavations at Christchurch College show that an artisan suburb was thriving outside the walls at the Abbey gate (**29**). What the quantity and distribution of pottery and small finds does reveal is the effect of the Viking raids: trade and population increase both here and within the city to the mid-800s, followed by diminished activity and a 30-year interruption in minting coins before final pre-Conquest revival.

27 *Saxon combs* c. 700–850. *These long-handled combs of fine workmanship are possibly Frisian and made of malleable antler horn with iron rivets.*

28 *Saxon coins* c. 710–40. *These proto-silver* sceattas *or pennies were probably minted in Kent, but not necessarily in Canterbury. One bears a porcupine design.*

29 *This tiny eighth-century decoration 2.4cm (1in) long was made for something bigger but never attached. Its interlaced animal design is a metal version of motifs found in church embroidery and calligraphy when Canterbury dominated south English styles. Covers for illuminated manuscripts, for instance, could have borne similar decoration.*

30 *Dated stylistically to the tenth century, this knife was probably made for a scribe in the Danish kingdom of York. Whether dropped by a Viking who first looted it or acquired by trade, it is finely decorated and has two folding blades – in the size and form of a modern pen-knife.*

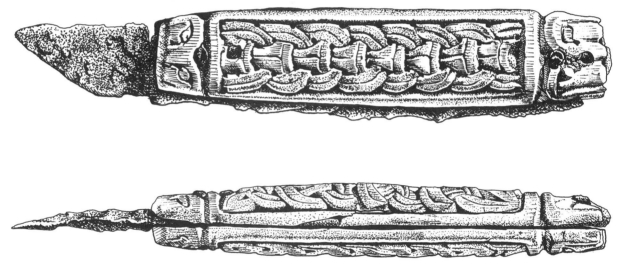

Danish Vikings

Canterbury, with some gains for great loss, survived the two waves of Viking attacks on Kent, between 835 and 855, and from 991 to 1012. 'Great slaughter' was recorded at Canterbury in 842, and in 851 when the Viking fleet was scattered by King Athelstan off Sandwich. Richly endowed coastal minsters from Hoo to Folkestone were sacked: the Abbess of Lyminge and probably nuns from Minster in Thanet established refuges in Canterbury. The combined minsters had owned a quarter of Kent's landed wealth but, by 1066, most had fallen to Christchurch, Canterbury or to the crown, only Dover, and St Augustine's still managing their own estates.

During the lull, Archbishop Oda raised and reroofed the Cathedral nave. The scriptorium was resurrected, from its nadir of one short-sighted scribe with small Latin and worse spelling, to produce, by 1020, dazzling manuscripts like Edui Basan's 'Arundel Psalter' (**30**). By this date Benedictine monks had finally replaced secular priests at the Cathedral. In 978 St Dunstan refounded the original and sole surviving East Kent abbey, adding St Augustine's name to its dedication. Its church was extended and successive reforming Abbots developed its library and scriptorium and built proper cloisters.

Almost annual raids from 991 to 1012 saw Danegeld screwed up from £10,000 to £48,000.

In 1009, Kent vainly paid £3000 to divert Thorkell's host elsewhere, for in 1011 they were back, demanding that Archbishop Alphege surrender the Cathedral treasures. For 20 days the citizens manned the Roman walls, until the Danes broke in when fire broke out. The *Anglo-Saxon Chronicle* accused Abbot Aelfmar of treachery, but with the newly-restored St Augustine's outside the walls, he may have struck some bargain to protect it. He was certainly 'allowed' to escape when the Archbishop, the King's Reeve, Abbess Leofrun and the Bishop of Rochester were all captured. The Cathedral, and most of the city was fired; its clergy and people killed, ransomed or enslaved and Alphege led off as hostage. When he forbade his people to raise additional ransom, he was killed with oxbones at a drunken feast at Greenwich. Yet Canterbury benefited from Cnut's contrition when, in 1023, his full court solemnly returned the sainted Alphege to a Cathedral shrine as important as St Dunstan's, accompanied by rich gifts and land grants. He

allowed St Augustine's to purloin St Mildred's remains from Minster in Thanet and a church was built or rededicated to her within Canterbury's walls near Worthgate (**31**).

The eve of the Conquest

Thanks to Domesday Book, Canterbury in 'the time of King Edward' can be reconstructed, with its 187 urban properties and 451 freemen burgesses. The total population is unknown although Osbern, the Christchurch monk, estimated it at 8000 during the Viking attack of 1011 (**32**). The King, Archbishop Stigand and Abbot Egelsin of St Augustine's were the prin-

31 *St Mildred's Church: the eleventh-century south wall. The only standing pre-Conquest parish church within the city walls retains 18.6m (61ft) of aisleless nave. The flint, tile and stone lying about after Viking attacks was consolidated by quoins of massive long and short stones. Cnut allowed St Augustine's Abbey to retrieve St Mildred's relics from her sacked nunnery at Minster, Thanet.*

cipal magnates, but Queen Edith and three local thegns also held jurisdiction. The city gild held 45 dwellings and 33 acres of land and witnessed property transactions. Town plots carried rights in the fields and water-meadows outside and for pig-pasture and wood-cutting. Supervising and adjudicating on these matters necessitated holding regular borough courts. Bruman, the King's Portreeve, oversaw the markets, except for St Augustine's Longport market and possibly one outside Westgate on the archbishop's land. He later acknowledged that he had taken tolls from foreign merchants rightfully belonging to the two religious houses. A string of markets from Wincheap round to Rithercheap, the cattle market, now lay outside the south-eastern wall circuit, as well as those within.

The town was divided into six wards called 'Berthae', based on the gates; by this means the defence of the walls was probably organized in 1011. Northgate and Westgate had churches above them, served by a gild of priests also tending St Dunstan's. St Mildred's may have served Worthgate and, although no formal parishes existed, the other three wards soon acquired Norman churches which could perhaps have pre-Conquest origins. Inhabitants of this thriving city, remembering recent Danish destruction, were not inclined to resist Duke William in 1066, despite the urgings of the Abbot of St Augustine's.

Topic: Canterbury's early churches

The six early churches strung out eastwards on their sites from the Cathedral to St Martin's have parallels at Glastonbury, Wells and Winchester but in number and date are remarkable (see **32**).

St Martin's (33)

The church lies north of three early Roman cremation cemeteries beside the road to Richborough. Nearby was found a second-century samian bowl, converted for later Christian use with a Chi-Rho graffito. The rectangular west end of the chancel is almost certainly Roman and stands 5m (16$\frac{1}{2}$ft) high with a south doorway leading to a small demolished porch. Late Christian 'built-tombs', used as shrines, occur near Dorchester, and a local fourth-century example survives at Stone-by-Faversham, outside the likely site of Durolevum.

Although archaeology cannot confirm this from associated remains, Ethelbert probably thought this was an old Christian building when he gave it to Queen Bertha and her chaplain Liudhart to restore before 597. Growing up in Tours, her devotion to St Martin was marked also at the Abbey, where she was buried, and at the north tower of the Saxon Cathedral. Augustine's monks who, according to Bede, used this church as their first missionary base, soon needed a larger building. When they extended it, they copied the building methods of their native Rome, as the seventh-century nave reveals in its fabric and its western windows. When their new Abbey was finished, they still used these methods for churches like Reculver. The settlement round the church expanded, despite the Danish raids, and included a body of clergy with a suffragan bishop or 'chorepiscopus' by 1035.

St Augustine's Abbey sites

The unexciting piles of stone here reveal more of the Abbey's early history than the continuously occupied Cathedral site can show. The first Norman Abbot, when levelling the Saxon works, respected old tombs, and their later removal to new shrines was faithfully recorded. Excavations in the 1930s laid bare the early church foundations and alterations within the skeleton of the Norman church, so that 942 years of change lie exposed.

32 *Topographical map of the city in 1050. Much of this is still conjectural, especially about the churches and in the area between the rivers where little archaeology has been possible. The road from Worthgate to the Cathedral is at this date as prominent as the High Street. Since this map was drawn the eleventh-century apse now alters the outline of the Cathedral.*

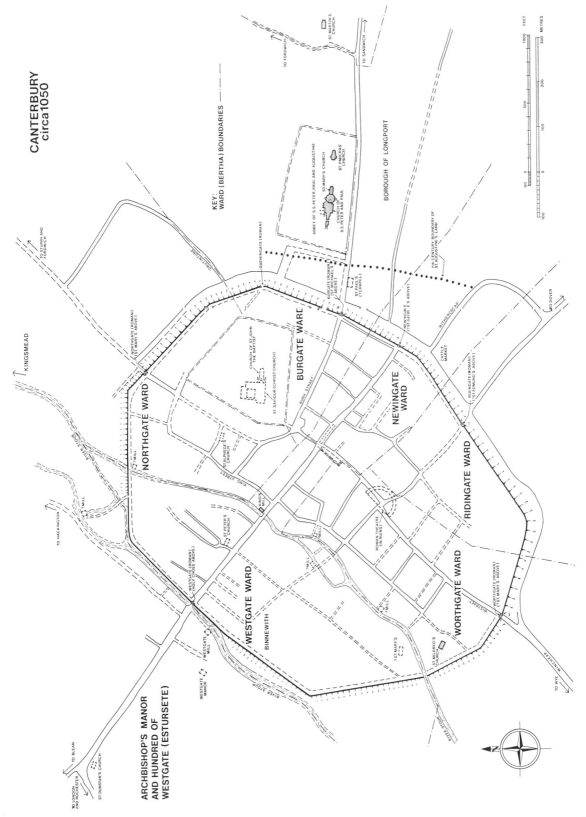

CANTERBURY
circa1050

KEY:
WARD (BERTHA) BOUNDARIES ------

ARCHBISHOP'S MANOR
AND HUNDRED OF
WESTGATE (ESTURSETE)

51

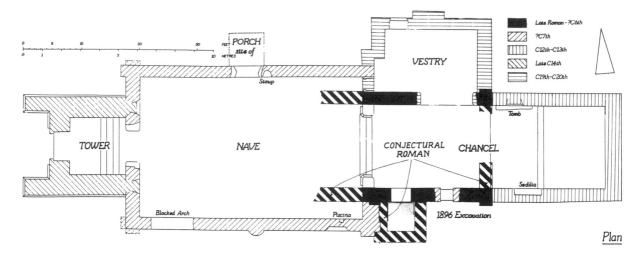

Plan

33 _Plan of St Martin's Church. The chancel's west end, of Roman brick, with original flat-headed south door, may be late fourth century, as Bede suggests; it was used by Queen Bertha before 597. The surviving nave walls contain rare ditrupa limestone from near Paris, perhaps sent, at Bertha's request, to aid Augustine's monks, building in late Roman style and reusing odd material, bonded with Roman brick._

Following Roman custom, archbishops and kings needed mausolea outside the walls, and here, from 598 to 613, Augustine's monks created the Abbey church of St Peter and St Paul. All their churches were small, about 12.5m (41ft) by 8.5m (28ft), and of similar form, with rectangular nave, apsidal east end, western narthex and a porticus north and south. Here, the north porticus of St Gregory contained the tombs of the first six archbishops; its later extension contained the remains of Abbot Hadrian and St Mildred, since, after 792, archbishops were buried at the Cathedral. The south porticus of St Martin contained royal graves until, about 620, after a brief apostasy, King Edbald, in penance, built a church to the Virgin, only 12.5m (41ft) to the east. Perhaps it had a similar south porticus for his own and subsequent royal burials, but only the west wall foundations and doorway of his church survive the creation of the Norman crypt, when these graves were moved to the Norman south transept.

The original church can never have been big enough for celebrations at this holiest Kentish shrine of the Canterbury saints. When St Dunstan rededicated it in 978, adding St Augustine's name, it was extended westwards by a second narthex and large vestibule. By the eleventh century, yet another chapel, with a possible western tower, stood west of the main church.

The fourth and most easterly church was dedicated to Pope Gregory's favourite child saint, Pancras. Today the only visible remains are several courses of well-laid Roman brick, the scars for its apsidal east end, its north and south chapels and an added west porch, still 3m (10ft) high. As at Reculver, a four-pillar colonnade divided apse from nave, of which one pillar survives. Continuing as a medieval lay cemetery chapel, its fourteenth-century east window was still reusing Roman bricks (**34**).

About 1050, Abbot Wulfric tried to rationalize the layout of his principal church. Visiting Reims, he had perhaps discussed the new continental fashion for rotundas, for he designed a two-storey rotunda to link St Mary's, as a new choir, to the original church, which would become the nave. He pushed ahead despite monastic doubts, but his death in 1059 was ascribed to divine judgement and the massive foundations and incomplete works

52

further determined Norman Abbot Scotland to start all over again.

Where and how the first monks lived is unknown. Excavations revealed the first cloister and associated buildings below their Norman successors. They seem to be eleventh-century and can probably be attributed to Abbot Aelfmar (1006–17) (**35**).

The first Cathedral

When, in January 1993, the first nave reflooring since 1787 and the renewal of central heating brought the Archaeological Trust to work within the Cathedral, knowledge of its Saxon evolution depended on a few documentary references and an elderly monk's memoirs. Eadmer was seven when fire destroyed the Cathedral in 1067, and over 60 when he wrote his recollections. Unconcerned with architecture, he sought to record and justify Canterbury cults in what he held to be Augustine's foundation. At the nave's west end he described the raised oratory of St Mary, containing the archbishop's *cathedra*. Celebrants faced east behind the altar, the congregation standing below, having entered past St Gregory's altar through the south tower, where a legal appeal court was held. The northern St Martin's tower served as a novice school. The apsidal eastern sanctuary with its principal shrines, including St Alphege, lay beyond the monk's choir at the nave's east end. It was raised over a crypt containing the special enclosure for St Dunstan's tomb. He recorded Lanfranc rebuilding 'from the very foundations' in seven years.

Documents record Archbishop Wulfred (803–13) 'renewing and restoring' the church at Canterbury and Oda (942–58) heightening and renewing the nave. St Dunstan's shrine in

34 *The ruins of St Pancras from the south. It is easier to visualize Augustine's first churches here, of square form with additions, north, south and west, and a shallow apse separated by a colonnade, the south pillar of which survives.*

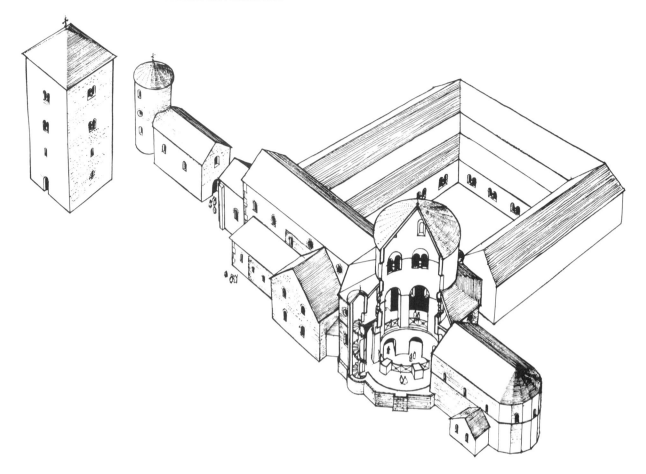

35 *Eleventh-century buildings at St Augustine's Abbey (conjectural). Land grants by Cnut had enriched the Abbey, while the Cathedral had gained an impressive continental-style western apse. Abbot Wulfric's octagonal rotunda on Burgundian lines would fittingly unite St Augustine's and King Edbald's seventh-century churches. After St Dunstan's restoration, the Abbey's scriptorium had European renown.*

the 980s altered the crypt, but it was unknown how often or extensively fire, risings and Viking raids had damaged the fabric. Digging to 44cm (17in) depth within the heating ducts was not expected to yield such dramatic phased results, corroborating much of Eadmer's account.

The archaeologists found two periods of rebuilding in the south aisle, revealing the longest Saxon Cathedral yet found. It had a squared western narthex and eastern foundations for a tower or choir which respected the

lines of the first church (see p.00). It is tempting to ascribe these remains to the recorded works of Wulfred and Oda.

After the Viking sack and the murder of Alphege one of the succeeding archbishops probably built the eleventh-century, deep western apse, so like contemporary German work, as at Trier (**colour plate 5**). Access to the Virgin's raised oratory was from a hexagonal stair tower found in Lanfranc's south aisle. A south-east tower was also added beside an earlier religious building of unknown use. Here perhaps was Eadmer's tower of St Gregory and appeal court (**36**). It is assumed that both these towers had northern counterparts, now lying below the cloisters.

Lanfranc worked from east to west after 1070 and his masonry showed a break before the stair turret. It seems that the newer western apse was demolished in a second phase, after acting as temporary home for the relics displaced by the building works. He obviously decided that the old south wall foundations would bear his arcade, but a new load-bearing wall was necessary further south. By moving the building over by 5m (16½ft) he incidentally won space to the north for his great cloister, below which the Saxon north wall must lie (see Topic: Chapter 4). Saxon builders had reused Roman stone, including massive blocks from some monumental building; this material was again incorporated in the Norman work. The bedding of Lanfranc's floor and some limestone paving blocks survive, still providing the solid base from which Yevele's fourteenth-century piers rise today.

St John the Baptist

Archbishop Cuthbert (740–60) built a church of unknown size and shape almost touching the east end of the Cathedral. It was a unique English purpose-built baptistery, although Cuthbert probably saw examples while visiting Rome. Apart from a font, a tank deep enough to let the accused sink during trials by ordeal must have existed, since Eadmer says that trials by ordeal under church supervision were conducted here. Since the building also stored books and charters and was the burial place of the archbishops after 792, there were probably also side chapels to serve these functions. It is not certain whether this building was demolished by Lanfranc or only under Anselm when the western crypt and great choir were constructed. Cuthbert was said to have obtained papal permission for burial within the city, as at contemporary Winchester. A cemetery south of the Cathedral existed by 1002 so funerals may also have been conducted there.

36 Saxon discoveries at the Cathedral. The remains found do not permit closer dating than the phases indicated. The monks' choir lay over the core of what now seems to be St Augustine's first church, until the great choir was completed in 1130; it is the site of today's nave altar.

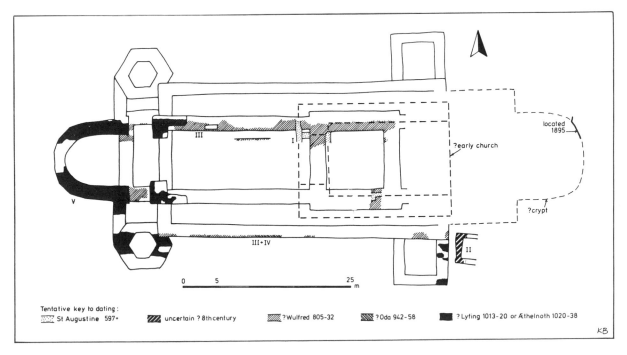

Tentative key to dating:
St Augustine 597+   uncertain ?8th century   ?Wulfred 805-32   ?Oda 942-58   ?Lyfing 1013-20 or Æthelnoth 1020-38

4

Norman builders

As they watched their Cathedral blazing in 1067 and recalled a year which had seen their king killed and William with his acquisitive retinue sweeping through Canterbury towards London, citizens could not foresee the century of unprecedented growth lying ahead, up to Becket's murder in 1170. Competitive builders at Cathedral and Abbey, and royal works at successive castles, were to create steady jobs for generations of building- and transport-workers and commercial opportunities for specialist craftsmen, shopkeepers and minters.

Canterbury is fortunate in its combination of documentary and archaeological evidence. Domesday Book describes minutely a fairly intact old order under new management, a picture corroborated by the monks' own Domesday record for Christchurch Priory of the 1090s and St Augustine's Abbey 'Excerpts', made for pursuing their own tenaciously held land rights. Prior Wibert's business acumen in the 1160s, mapping his water system and listing, swapping and extending urban properties, provided further documents for Dr William Urry (**colour plate 6**). His pioneering *Canterbury under the Angevin Kings* compiled one of the earliest detailed maps of a Norman city. Archaeological work at Canterbury's castles, in the precincts and at the Archbishop's Palace throws light on major buildings initiated before Domesday Book; excavations at St Gregory's Priory and St John's Hospital confirm Lanfranc's towering reputation. The wealth, status

and international trade of Canterbury's richer citizens was illuminated by discoveries below the Longmarket, while widely separated small sites across the city revealed the homes and workshops of humbler citizens. Research on the human bones from St Gregory's cemetery is gradually demonstrating the diet, diseases and life expectancy of the whole spectrum of local society (**37**).

Royal possessions

Three wedges of land surrounded the central core of the city. The king's land lay south and east, St Augustine's Abbey's east and north and that of the archbishop and his monks north and west.

Royal land outside the walls contained four later small manors and the lands of the burgess gild. In addition, Kingmead Road today probably traverses the eight acres of meadow recorded in Domesday Book, reserved for the use of royal messengers, where 'the King's horses graze while coming and going'; he also owned three of the area's 38 watermills. King's Mill stood beside the Eastbridge in the High Street until the eighteenth century. Hamo the Sheriff collected £54 in tax, roughly the same as Bruman, his Saxon predecessor. Despite the razing of 60 houses for the castles and Archbishop's Palace, about 200 houses lay inside and outside the walls; 451 burgesses are enumerated, of whom the king controlled 263, the archbishop 116 and the abbot of St Augus-

tine's 70. These figures suggest a population of about 3000. The monastic communities and the unpropertied poor can perhaps double this number. Yet, from the Black Death to 1750, Canterbury's population was smaller and today its Domesday size has only increased sixfold.

William I immediately ordered a motte and bailey castle, utilizing, as at Pevensey, Roman remains. A dig in 1981 in Dane John gardens (Norman Donjon) discovered a huge ditch 3m (10ft) deep, backfilled in the twelfth century, containing waterlogged organic material possibly from the original palisade atop the bailey bank. Absence of other Norman material suggests the topsoil was moved to consolidate the Roman burial mound as a motte (**38**). An equally massive ditch appeared in two places outside the city wall near the East Station in 1988–9. It seems likely that the motte stood in a figure-of-eight bailey each side of the dilapidated Roman city wall. By the 1200s,

37 *St Gregory's cemetery and Trevor Anderson (bone specialist). When analysed, the 1350 skeletons interred between 1086 and 1537 should become the type-site for medieval bone studies. Priory canons, local artisans and hospital residents surviving earlier fractures and disease, provide a large, mixed sample over a long period.*

Dane John manor lay across the extramural part. Shifting castles was not uncommon and a charter of 1095 proves that a '*castellum novum*' already existed on the site of the present stone castle, a more strategic situation between the river and the Roman gate towards Hythe. The *Anglo-Saxon Chronicle* relates how, in September 1089, some of St Augustine's monks organized a sit-down strike at St Mildred's church outside the castle, on behalf of brothers imprisoned for opposing Lanfranc's new Abbot Wydo. Only hunger dispersed the protesters.

Stylistically, the replacement stone keep compares with Bamburgh and Corfe. Probably begun when the archbishopric was vacant between 1109 and 1114, it must have been complete when Henry I, to mollify Archbishop William de Corbeil for this insulting local innovation, asked him to build a modernized keep at Rochester Castle in 1127. At 30m (98ft) by 26m (85ft) Canterbury is smaller than Colchester, but comparable with Kenilworth and Taunton. It was a stylish construction on three floors, of bonded ragstone, with an elaborate Quarr stone plinth and Caen stone dressings. Anticipating royal visits, several well-lit upper rooms were provided with chimneys and a well shaft to all floors (**39**). The keep was continually repaired up to 1271 and extended by a barbican, but only battered remains

38–39 *Canterbury's Norman Castles: 1066 and 1123. The first castle utilized a Roman mound, but was soon re-sited further round the Roman wall circuit. The stone castle later replaced the probable second version. Archbishop de Corbeil further refined this design at Rochester after 1127.*

survive today, thanks to its usefulness as a coke store when the gasworks occupied the site.

The king's remarkable half-brother Odo, Bishop of Bayeux, as Kent's earl, owned numerous city properties attached to his rural manors, and in addition cut a 300-acre deer-park from land above Fordwich. Three of his principal vassals disputed other properties with the burgesses, while another acquired four dwellings owned by King Harold's concubine. Canterbury's strongest link with Odo may be the Bayeux Tapestry itself, in which he and two of his Kentish knights feature prominently. Professor Brooks suggests that working its 70.75m (232ft) length was possibly supervised at St Augustine's where the Bishop was on cordial terms with the Abbot. It went to Bayeux forever in 1082.

St Augustine's Abbey

Abbot Scotland, arriving at Lanfranc's invi-

tation from Mont St Michel in 1070, at once reclaimed most of Fordwich, Canterbury's port, which had been given away to Hamo the Sheriff. Odo of Bayeux surrendered the rest and through this little port Caen stone arrived in huge quantities. From 1073 to his death in 1087, Scotland, with papal permission, demolished seventh-century St Mary's Church to rebuild a splendid apsidal east end to the Abbey church on a matching crypt. In 1091, the first Saxon church and its porticuses were demolished and at a magnificent public ceremony, specially recorded by Goscelin, Bishop Gundulf of Rochester initiated the translation of St Augustine, his successors, and St Mildred to their new shrines round the high altar. St Augustine's Abbey's uniquely ancient status was reasserted and points were scored in the running battle with the Cathedral and St Gregory's Priory over the relative importance of their relics and the custody of St Mildred.

Building funds came largely from the Abbey's 280 ploughlands and numerous advowsons spread by royal gift across Kent since the seventh century. The manor of Longport encircled the Abbey between the Sandwich and Dover roads. Today's orchards towards Patrixbourne cover the lands of 91 Domesday tenants; St Lawrence cricket ground covers the Abbey's leper hospital and the demesne, or Barton, still contains Barton Court School. Their 70 burgesses lived near the Abbey's Longport market, beside the modern coach park where tourists cross to the gardens covering the lay cemetery. Domesday Book mentions four nuns holding land from the Abbot; the origin of St Sepulchre's nunnery, founded under Anselm by the son-in-law of Vitalis, a vassal of Odo appearing in the Bayeux Tapestry. It survived on the corner of Oaten Hill as a poor Benedictine house of eight nuns until the Dissolution.

Archbishop's land

The dynamic Italian sexagenarian, Archbishop Lanfranc, apart from reorganizing the English Church, advising his king and building compulsively (see Topic) was primarily a monk. By expanding Christchurch Priory to 150 monks, he aimed to provide a reservoir of spiritual talent to energize the church. For their support he divided his estates with his monks, who owned 200 acres running along the Stour from Northgate and curling eastwards round the boundaries of Lanfranc's new foundations at St Gregory's and St John's. The manor comprised a vineyard, water meadows, outlying swine pasture, demesne land and eight mills, of which Barton Mill still operates today; 97 burgesses lived around Northgate and 33 tenants towards Sturry.

The archbishopric acquired the famous vill of St Martin's from Saxon kings in the tenth century. The Wic trading settlement, stretching towards Fordwich, had withered under Viking attacks to a village round the church; it supported 44 peasant families and was split between the archbishop and his tenant Ralph the Chamberlain. On the west of the city the archbishop's large manor of Estursete or Westgate stretched towards Blean forest's pig pastures, but also contained 100 acres of meadow, 12 mills along the river and supported 20 plough teams.

Parish churches

Modern Canterbury has six functioning parish churches and three with new roles. Surprisingly, two are certainly and three possibly pre-Conquest and four are Norman. Norman dynamism created formal parishes and increased these figures to 22 before the Black Death began the long decline in numbers.

Apart from Saxon St Martin and St Mildred, the foundation charter of St Gregory's Priory, though suspect in date, mentions St Mary above Northgate, Holy Cross above Westgate and St Dunstan outside Westgate. St Andrew in the main street and St Mary de Castro were exchanged by William I with St Augustine's for land for his second castle. St Alphege is possibly and St George is probably pre-Conquest; St Peter and St Paul are not much later.

Odo's knight Vitalis built St Edmund Ridingate; his son, Hamo, the wooden church of St Mary 'Bredin'. Its city-centre successor, bombed in 1942, was moved and thrives today opposite the nunnery site founded by Hamo's brother-in-law, William Caudwell. Six more city churches, and two at Burgate and Queningate, arose in the following century. St John Baptist and St Helen were relatively short-lived but All Saints and St Mary Bredman survived to this century; their High Street sites are marked. St Mary Magdalen's tower still stands in Burgate and St Margaret's now houses the 'Canterbury Tales' experience.

The survivors are mainly built of flint, ragstone and reused Roman brick and on their cramped sites are never orientated eastwards. Whether moved, expanded or truncated by eighteenth-century 'improvers' they have served close-knit neighbourhoods for nearly 900 years. Dr Urry found mention of over 70 twelfth-century priests and clerks; many were married and passed on their jobs like 'Soloman the Priest, son of Osbert the Priest'.

The city centre

Some suburbs were more populous than in the early nineteenth century, straggling for half a mile beyond Northgate, Westgate and Worthgate and stretching along the eastern edge from the Cattlemarket to Northgate. This reflected housing density within the walls. Up to 200 shops existed; the owners of large properties divided them into seven-foot shop frontages along Burgate, the High Street and adjoining lanes. Godwin Mercer made eight units from his holding, while the west side of Mercery Lane held a stone house divided into six shops and a wooden one split between three. Thirty-seven shops lined Burgate while Susanna de Planaz owned nine High Street shops. At least 30 stone houses existed by 1200, some underpinned by stone cellars still found below modern shops. Goods were made in workshops and backyards and sold from counters outside. Trades were seldom clustered together, except for the North Lane tanners beside the river and 11 leather workers in a sub-divided property in the Corvisery near Butchery Lane.

In 1990, excavations ahead of the second redevelopment of Longmarket since its wartime destruction, provided a fascinating correlation between history and archaeology. Christchurch Priory owned approaching one half of the city's property by 1200. From rent-rolls and surveys Dr Urry located most of the Longmarket area's property boundaries. These were found as fairly permanent topographical features, with masonry walls surviving until 1942 (**40**).

Some of Canterbury's wealthiest citizens lived here, chief of whom was Theoric the Goldsmith, for a time Borough Reeve. He set up a Royal Exchange, acted as agent for kings Richard and John and employed day-labourers. Parts of his family stone house were found in 1946 on the north-east of the site. He also occupied the opposite corner, once Sunwin's smithy, where a possibly contemporary large masonry building was traced. Along Sunwin's (now Butchery) Lane, Theoric had yet another holding, connected to the rear of his family property by a cellared masonry building of possible early thirteenth-century date. Due to the frequent rebuilding of this prime site over centuries and the multitude of backyard cess- and rubbish pits, the cut-about remains are exceptionally difficult to interpret. A tempting discovery was the disturbed building behind Theoric's home, where burnt clay floors contained traces of ovens, furnaces, ceramic crucibles and metalworking debris (**41** and **42**). Whatever Theoric's impact, archaeology revealed extensive rebuilding in the prosperous mid-thirteenth century, with substantial timber-framed houses on masonry cellars and undercrofts. Thousands of sherds from rubbish pits are being examined, some to reveal high-

quality tableware and decorated jugs from Germany, France, Spain, North Africa and the Middle East. Cess-pit analysis may reveal what these dishes contained.

Besides Theoric, 11 more goldsmiths worked in Canterbury between 1149 and 1200. Canterbury was also second only to London in its eight mints and quantity of coin struck. The king, the archbishop and St Augustine's all operated mints (**43**). A William I penny, minted by Winedi in 1087, was found in Burgate Lane near a property occupied by 'William, son of Winedi'. The names of Gregory, Robert, Soloman, Luke, Wiulph, Freawin, Ollard and Ordlief appear as minters alongside Maynier the Rich, whose twelfth-century Hospital still houses almspeople. Lambin Frese was paid ten marks by Christchurch to move his mint from the city centre, probably after the Cathedral fire of 1174. He set up on the river bank in a stone building, later a Hospital for Poor Priests, where excavation discovered Frese's original floor. Two custodians, a clerk and their servants lived at the Royal Exchange, marked by a plaque near the Post Office. Enough minters occupied sites opposite to give the name of 'The Mint' to modern Whitehorse Lane.

Here too, until their expulsion in 1290, lived Canterbury's Jews, along Stour Street to what is still called Jewry Lane. When they went, 13 houses were sold. Jacob's stone house on the east corner of Stour Street, with the synagogue behind, was rented from Christchurch Priory, with which relations were cordial. During the 19 months in 1188 to 1189 when the monks were sequestered in the precincts during their dispute with Archbishop Baldwin, the Jews smuggled in food for them. In a farcical episode, the cellarer, Norreys, escaped through the monastic sewer, to be installed as Prior by Baldwin. Richard I had to come in person to oblige the archbishop to abandon his plans for a college of secular canons and dismiss Norreys. Perhaps this affected the £235 Canterbury Jews contributed towards Richard's later ransom, half the sum coming from Jacob himself.

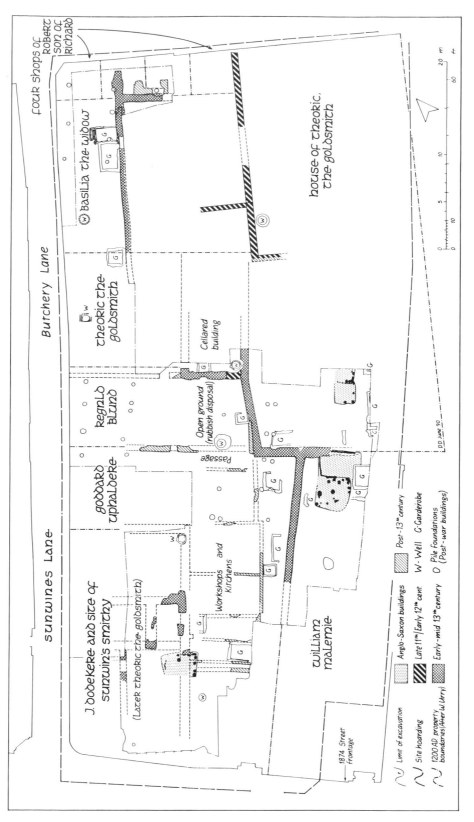

Sunwines Lane

Butchery Lane

four shops of Robert son of Richard

Basilia the widow

Theoric the goldsmith

house of Theoric, the goldsmith

Regnld Blind

Goddard Uphalbere

J. Dodekere and site of Sunwin's smithy

(Later Theoric the goldsmith)

Workshops and Kitchens

Cellared building

Open ground (rubbish disposal)

Passage

William Malemie

1874 Street frontage

DD June 90

Limit of excavation

Site hoarding

1200 AD property boundaries (After W. Urry)

Anglo-Saxon buildings

Late 11th / Early 12th cent.

Early-mid 13th century

Post-13th century

W - Well   G - Garderobe

O Pile Foundations (Post-war buildings)

20 m

60 ft

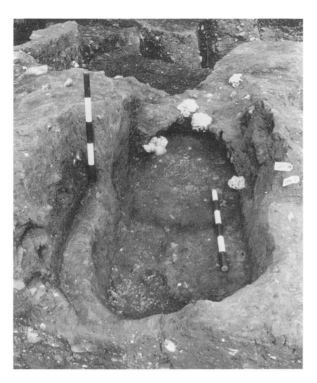

40–42 *Longmarket properties, furnace and crucibles, c. 1200. Cathedral priory rent rolls and archaeology combine in this map. Land to the rear of Theoric the goldsmith's properties, although badly disturbed, revealed extensive burnt clay flooring, traces of ovens, furnaces, metal working debris and ceramic crucibles (**41** and **42**).*

43 *A long cross penny from William I's last issue of 1087, minted by Winedi a Canterbury moneyer, was found in the backfill of an early Norman rubbish pit. The industrial site, used for iron smelting since the tenth century, later became a bell-foundry.*

Cathedral and city

Monks and citizens were closely bound together. Many rented property from Christchurch; or were like William Drogoson, who received one penny way-leave for the monks' waterpipe to cross his land. Monks like Gervase the Chronicler or Theoric the Goldsmith's son brought in properties on their profession. Many maintained the precinct buildings: seven masons, eight carpenters, five painters, two thatchers and a glazier feature in the accounts beside Ingenulph the Plumber, whose annual wage was 25 shillings, although his wife made a useful £8 selling ale to the monks.

A hierarchy of 100 servants tended a monastic community not much larger, from the sacristy servers down to Sired Scutellarius, who washed up the refectory dishes, and the washerwoman and drain cleaner who got free meals on their weekly visits. Osbert Vinitor had a house, winepress and toolstore at Coldharbour beyond Northgate, near John the monastic cook. Malger and William, porters at the gates, were allowed to sell for themselves the dung they cleared behind visitors' horses. Reginald and Walter ran the Brewhouse, now part of the King's School. The adjoining Archbishop's Palace had its own staff. The Arch-

bishop's kitchen, now a Palace Street shop, was financed from his own coastal Borough of Seasalter. Godwin the Stabler lived near the Archbishop's stables, briefly revealed in a dig below sheltered housing in Staplegate. This area remained for centuries outside city jurisdiction, a twilight zone of shady inhabitants. Norman paupers, however, lived outside the walls, sending their offspring seasonally to work on the land, to beg at monastery gates or do the thankless jobs in the city. Lodderer, or Beggars', Lane lay outside Newingate and Un-thankesway outside Northgate.

Other citizens were outside purveyors of corn, fodder, cloth and fine wines to the monks. Godefrid the Baker, whose family appears in an early Becket miracle, lived near Palace Street. A small dig inside Westgate revealed the unique kiln of an immigrant Norman potter (**44**). Distinctive ware, greatly superior to the local product, was found near the *Aula Nova* guest hall in the precincts, and was thought to have been imported until similar goods appeared in this kiln. The potter may not have been the only stranger attracted by the custom of two great religious houses. Local craftwork appears regularly at city sites, such as locks, a fine mace-head and delicately carved bone and ivory. Three sites have yielded substantial Norman hall-houses. By 1200, documentary evidence attests well-populated streets on both sides of the river's eastern branch. This unhealthy area was prone to flooding, a problem increased by the large number of watermills, and must have housed the poorer citizens. Apart from a long-established bakery found in Stour Street, few chances to excavate have arisen in this area, where a high water-table should allow the survival of the more ephemeral traces of the poor.

Prior Wibert continued the work in the precincts begun by Lanfranc. His hand in the 1160s is visible everywhere – at the Water Tower, the infirmary chapel and cloister, the treasury and the Great Gate and *Aula Nova* (**colour plates 6** and **7**), a final flowering of

1 Central Durovernum c.300. Area excavation of the Roman city was possible because redevelopment of central bomb sites was so long delayed. Evidence to reconstruct the Temple precinct emerged on five sites, phases of the bath-house on three sites and earlier sightings of the massive theatre were confirmed. Domestic housing, successively upgraded, often included private baths. Evidence of activity into the fifth century also appeared.

2   *Roman Riding Gate. This took its name from the red bonding-courses of an impressive flint and greensand gate comprehensively excavated in 1986, for the third time. The Dover road ran through it. Stone plinths, held with iron clamps, supported the double-arched gate, flanked by two guardrooms. Wooden doors led to a bridge over the ditch.*

3   *Riding Gate details. Iron hinges, a worn socket and the nails securing the south door's bottom beam survived just below the modern roadway. The iron clamp joining the central plinth appears top left.*

4 *Central Cantwaraburh c.650. Saxon huts were found on Whitefriars in 1960 but the mid-seventh-century sunken huts near the ruined Theatre revealed the revival after the Cathedral was built. Some sheltered in courtyards or by walls or used road foundations, so altering the street pattern. A late Roman burial was found where sheep graze on the Temple site.*

5 *Eleventh-century western apse: Cathedral 1993. The curve of the apse lies between the present west and north doors of the Cathedral. Lanfranc's later nave was moved southwards. The fourteenth-century pier to the right of the font rests on Lanfranc's paving.*

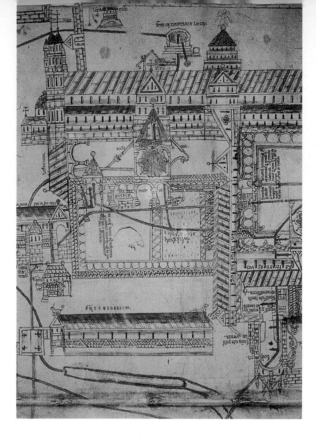

6a *Prior Wibert's waterworks, 1140 (after Willis' redrawing). Skilful management of centralized finances provided money for building and ambitious hydraulics. Tapping five springs, water was piped through six settling tanks and the city wall to the tower in the Infirmary cloister whence it flowed by gravity throughout the enclosure.*

6b *Aula Nova and Gate, 1140. The system ended above the staircase to Wibert's great hall and new gate. The red drain, still accessible, flowed under the precinct and city walls into the yards of Broad Street smithies and was cleaned weekly.*

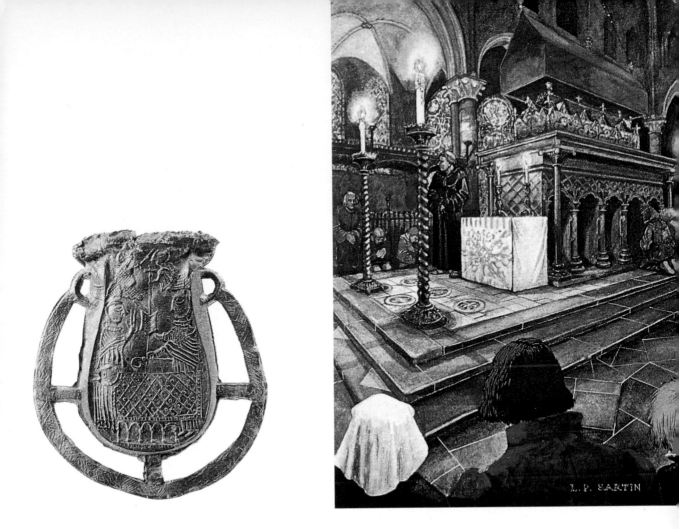

8a Pilgrim ampulla c1225-50 (8.2cm (3½in) high): reverse. This tin bottle for holy water could be hung round a pilgrim's neck. Its mould was found in Watling Street. The front shows Becket and a Latin jingle, 'Thomas is the best doctor of the worthy sick.'

8b Reconstruction view of Becket's Shrine. One window in the Trinity Chapel and a fire-damaged sketch in the Cotton MSS are the only surviving images of the Shrine. The pavement with its zodiac circles remains, resembling contemporaries at Westminster. Sick pilgrims could crouch within the arched base. At its destruction in 1538, two chests containing the best jewels, including Louis VII's great ruby last seen in Mary I's collar, accompanied 26 other cartloads to London.

7 Aula Nova and Gate today. The King's School funded an excavation revealing the missing half of the Aula Nova, demolished in 1730. It was the school's second home before 1566 when it moved to the Mint Yard. Under it lay a possible mint weight of William I. Prior Chillenden altered the gate in about 1390.

9 *Central Canterbury's pilgrim inns 1520. From the corner in the bottom centre a surprising amount of this view is still visible, despite altered facades, particularly the right corner of the huge 'Cheker' and Prior Goldwell's Christchurch Gate, replacing the cemetery gate visible to the right of the 'Sun'. Vanished casualties are St Andrew's, High Street (1763), St Mary Bredman (bottom left) (1900) and the Guildhall (far left) (1950).*

10 High Street, 1827, by Sidney Cooper. Ward's print shows the Royal Mail coach from Paris leaving the Coach and Horses (now the Royal Museum 1897). The Paving Commissioners had widened the bridge, removed All Saint's tower, refaced Eastbridge Hospital and installed lighting, already converted for burning gas from the Castle works. The weavers' houses still stand.

11 Opening Day: Canterbury to Whitstable Railway May 1830. Ward's print was issued as an advertisement to innkeepers. A winding engine, not a locomotive, is hauling the carriages by cable up the incline from North Lane Station to the tunnel entrance. Smeaton's mill, standing before the Cathedral, and the oast demonstrate the agricultural produce the railway's backers hoped to move profitably.

12 The city from the University of Kent. Prehistoric man and modern student could look from this tertiary terrace to the opposite one across the Stour flood-plain. Holford's colleges frame this view from their halls which lie over the railway tunnel approached in colour plate 11. The gateway of St Augustine's Abbey stands east of the Cathedral.

late Romanesque before the French Gothic of William of Sens from 1176.

Topic: Lanfranc the Builder

Lanfranc's work at Canterbury makes sense in the context of his Norman past and his aims as Archbishop. Appointed Abbot of William's new monastery of St Etienne, Caen, Lanfranc had begun that magnificent Romanesque church in 1064. Arriving reluctantly in August 1070 for his consecration in the fire-damaged nave at Canterbury, he brought his prior, Gundulf, with him. The speed and scale of their nave rebuilding, revealed in 1993, is described in Topic: Chapter 3. When, in 1077, the work at Caen and its copy at Canterbury were completed Gundulf became Bishop of Rochester, there to build a monastic cathedral, start the castle and supervise William's 'White Tower' in London. His Canterbury work was recorded recently when archaeologists found

44 *A kiln and rouletted pot from Pound Lane. The oldest medieval Kentish kiln yet found yielded pottery, dated 1150–75, previously thought to be northern French imports, when discovered at Precincts sites. These wares were better refined, thrown, decorated and fired than contemporary Tyler Hill wares; inferior local copies, possibly ten years later, were found on other sites.*

Norman buttresses and 24.6m (81ft) of the crossing piers still sustaining the central tower. The west wall of the crypt, embodying two columns with the earliest English cushion capitals, is early work exposed in the crypt Treasury.

Within fifty years all 15 English cathedrals were rebuilt on grander and uniform lines, and eight had become monastic institutions. This vision dictated the scale of Lanfranc's redesigned priory buildings and despite frequent refurbishments, his Great Cloister retains its spacious Lanfranc dimensions (**45**). The undercroft and one wall of his massive dormitory survive, accommodating the modern library in one-third of its area. He also initiated the Infirmary Hall, the 1100 arcade of which remains; even medieval monks found it overlarge, carving a subprior's lodging from its south aisle. Domesday Book records that 27 houses were destroyed for the Archbishop's '*Nova hospitatio*', set in a three-acre precinct, created in the city centre by pushing the road to Northgate westwards; Lanfranc's legacy is the awkward double bend from Palace Street today.

Contemporary accounts of Becket's murder describe the Great Hall, flanked by a northern porch, western kitchen and the archbishop's private chambers and chapel eastwards. In 1985, Mrs Runcie's new garden project exposed a wing of this palace running northwards, probably for the archbishop's household (**46**). Archaeologists found the undercroft at its southern end. Further study of the modern Palace, incorporating Elizabethan Archbishop Parker's alterations, revealed Lanfranc's building, 32m (105ft) by 10m (33ft), made of flint and Roman brick set in yellowish mortar. Two original doors and windows with Quarr stone jambs were exposed. Traces of original external plaster indicated that the aisled upper storey overhung an arcade leading to a private court adjoining the west cloister buildings. Drawings of Lanfranc's north-west tower, replaced after 1832, show a first-floor door allowing the archbishop direct access to the west end of the

Cathedral, where his *cathedra* perhaps stood, to hear his monks sing the offices.

Before 1085 Lanfranc turned his energies to charity. Healthily outside the city on his Westgate manor at Harbledown, Lanfranc founded St Nicholas' Leper Hospital, this dedication perhaps commemorating the arrival of the saint's remains at Bari in 1087. Lanfranc ordered 'skilful, patient and kindly watchers' to tend male and female lepers in wattle huts round the church on its knoll. The mainly twelfth-century chapel with Norman arcading has lost its original apse. The hospital still houses almspeople, its role since leprosy died out. He also dedicated a hospital for 30 men and 30 women to St John the Baptist, on whose decapitation feast day he became bishop. For its ninth centenary, the Archaeological Trust surveyed and cleared the remains of his 61.5m (202ft) double dormitory. At the northern

45 *Lanfranc and his Cathedral. The 1993 nave excavations largely confirmed the accuracy of this earlier model. The larger cloister and dormitory for the expanded priory of 150 monks were by-products of moving the nave southwards by the width of the south aisle.*

end three flint walls survive to the first floor, containing a door with original timber lintel and a spiral stair (**47**). One wall at the southern end is incorporated in the present hospital hall. Of the two privy blocks lying behind, the northern survived in continuous use to 1948; now restored, it explains Norman sanitary engineering. Thick walls with five windows enclosed an area 10.5m (34$\frac{1}{2}$ft) by 2.65m (9ft), above a deep masonry-lined pit with five arches for ventilation and flushed by roof rainwater. Drains, probably from a possible kitchen block,

crossed the orchard, only severed from Lanfranc's foundation in 1991 for a car-park. The twin-aisled church projected eastwards from the dormitory range but was fire-damaged in the fourteenth century; one Norman doorway survives. Opposite, the archbishop provided a new house of canons to care for his old people.

The way in which he regularized the life and status of local priests is seen when Domesday Book in 1086 records property held by 'the clergy of the town in their guild'; St Gregory's Priory charter details identical property held

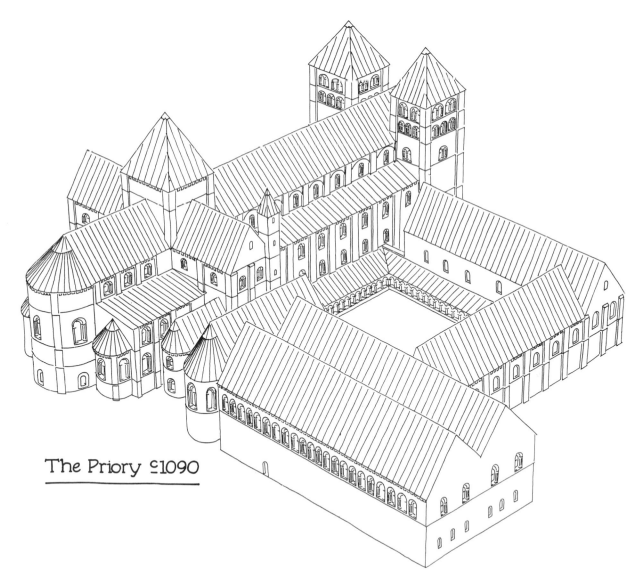

The Priory c1090

by 'the clergy of St Gregory for their church'. They continued to serve three city churches and the nearby cemetery, while also tending the almsfolk across the road. Cemetery, priory and successive churches were all excavated in 1988–9 (**48**). William de Corbeil, first Augustinian Archbishop, possibly converted Lanfranc's house of secular canons into a Regular Augustinian house after 1123. Burnt down soon after, Lanfranc's church was enlarged and rebuilt by Archbishop Theobald (1139–61)

46 *Lanfranc's Palace from the Cathedral north-west tower. The close relationship of Palace and Cathedral is clear. The Hall continued westwards across the drive. Forming a T with it lay Lanfranc's household apartments, incorporated in the 1899 Palace.*

47 *St John's Hospital dormitory 1084–1984. Unlike Lanfranc's Priory, his old peoples' hospital survived the Dissolution and continues today under the Archbishop's patronage. This northern end of the flint dormitory and its unique reredorter were cleared by the Trust and can be visited.*

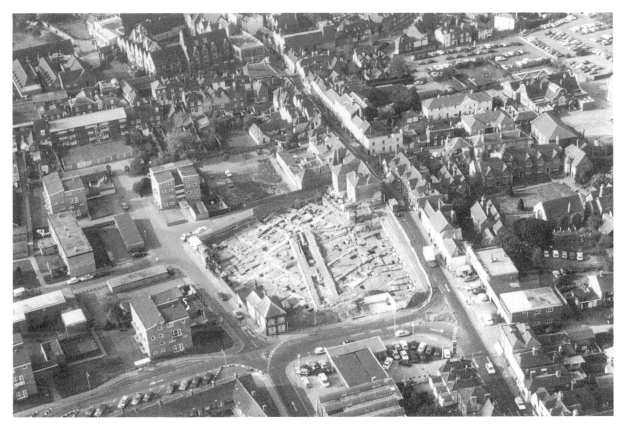

who completed the claustral buildings appearing in Wibert's 1160s' waterworks drawing. In return for piped water, the canons gave an annual basket of apples to Christchurch. The precinct also contained the archdeacon's house and chapel.

The mutilated remains of Lanfranc's priory church are enigmatic. By the 1145 fire, a rectangular nave, square tower and chancel were flanked by transepts containing eastward projecting two-cell chapels. The later transepts, differently constructed, abutted massive nave foundations; the two chapels and chancel were different again, with well-squared Caen and Quarr stone blocks. Floor sequences do not aid dating but bear evidence of the fire. Documents record that in 1085 Lanfranc brought the remains of St Ethelburga and St Mildred from Lyminge to his new foundation on St

48 Aerial view of St Gregory's Priory and St John's Hospital. Most of the excavated Augustinian church overlying Lanfranc's original has the cloister to the right, marred by parallel GPO foundations and the cemetery to the left. Over the road, later hospital cottages and the surviving quarter of the chapel surround the close. The hall and stair turret were adapted from the south end of the Lanfranc dormitory; the north end is shown in 47. Post-war council flats replaced army terraces across the Priory land.

Augustine's doorstep. As that Abbey also claimed possession of St Mildred since Cnut's reign, Lanfranc would have ordered lavish chapels for these prestigious relics. It seems, therefore, that an early church, flanked by two free-standing chapels, was subsequently amalgamated by linking the chapels with transepts to a lengthened nave.

5
'Holy, blissful martyr'?

From Becket to Henry VIII, Canterbury seems to reach its peak as a splendid magnet for pilgrims, akin to Rome and Compostella. In fact, records and standing archaeology show Canterbury, like other towns, growing its own identity as the economic, legal and political focus of its region, similarly affected by national events and that natural disaster, the Black Death.

Expansion 1220–1348

Mirroring national figures, Canterbury's population grew from 6000 to 10,000, pulling in people from 30 miles around and short-stay migrants from far afield. Rentals show density increasing as properties were subdivided, but people were unevenly spread. The populous poor lived outside Northgate and in the southern quarter and its adjacent suburbs. The rich lived at the top end of town round the precincts, while the riverside area lay undeveloped, except for watermills, until the Friars arrived. Merchants built solid houses, bought leases and tenements, but still lived alongside back lane shacks.

Archbishop Becket's murder by Henry II's knights in the late afternoon of Tuesday 29 December 1170, in his own Cathedral, is the best-documented event in English medieval history. In life, the monks of Canterbury had distrusted Thomas, the king's servant, advanced with indecent haste from minor orders to archbishopric. They felt his bitter

quarrel with the king and six-year exile were self-inflicted and left them unsupported and the city harried by his enemies. His sacrilegious death transformed their attitude. The monks were astounded to discover a hair shirt and monastic habit under their worldly archbishop's vestments. The citizens witnessed the murder, scrabbled for blood-soaked relics from his corpse and attested an early miracle, when poor Manwin's sight was restored by a drop of the martyr's blood begged from a neighbour. William, the monastic 'watcher', recorded that 'the city of Canterbury which knows that he was blind before, knows equally well that he afterwards regained his sight'. God's hand was seen in 1174, in Henry II's public penance here and when, that September, fire gutted the choir but spared the saint's body in the crypt.

The next fifteen brilliant years saw Canterbury the centre of English and European religious life. Books on Becket and his miracles, the building of the revolutionary Gothic Choir, the restoration of Cathedral rights and city prosperity went hand in hand. In July 1220 St Thomas was at last 'translated' to his new Cathedral shrine in the Trinity chapel, with Archbishop Stephen Langton presiding over a star-studded royal and ecclesiastical cast. This festival started a tradition of royal visits and a new Canterbury Calendar of saints' days and anniversaries, bringing wealth 'by the liberality and expence of such as gadded to St Thomas for help and devotion', as Lambarde later described (see **colour plate 8**). In time, Edward, the Black Prince, and then a contrite Henry IV, the deposer of his son, came to lie each side of Becket's shrine in splendid tombs. The precincts filled with buildings, shrewd property management increased the Priory's income, so that domestic and construction jobs, and commissions for luxury objects came the citizens' way.

Adjacent estates, hospitals and parish churches benefited, while active demesne farming produced surpluses for city markets and fairs. The arrival of Friars inflated the numbers of religious, so encouraging a new professional class of lay and ecclesiastical lawyers, land agents and financiers. By 1300, Canterbury hosted diplomatic visits, legal sessions and parliamentary elections and had retained its mints when Henry I closed other Kentish centres. Until 1335, nearly every issue was struck here: minting only ended in 1549. Goldsmithing flourished along with the base-metal trade in pilgrim badges (**49**). Moulds are found here and badges and *ampullae* have been discovered across Europe. East Kent wool and grain were exported to Flanders and business links established with north Italian cities.

The Friaries 1221–1500

Whether tackling urban poverty and disease, or doubt and ignorance, the new Franciscan and Dominican orders targeted the same fifty or so English county, university and cathedral towns: Canterbury was an obvious starting point. The Dominicans preached before Stephen Langton in 1221 and founded their eleventh English house here in 1236, while the Franciscans arrived, during St Francis' lifetime, in 1224. Hoping to avoid the perils of wealth, they begged for necessities and persuaded benefactors to administer their properties. Merchant patrons usually found them poor peripheral land, but Canterbury's Grey and Black Friars had precincts within the walls, by the river; their topographical effect was to close off existing lanes (see **10**). As elsewhere, only

49 *Often regarded as secondary relics themselves, pilgrim badges such as this, approximately 5cm (2in) tall, were cast in thousands in silver, lead or latten, an alloy, and are often found along with swords, murder scenes and ampullae at other shrines, like Walsingham. This popular memento of the jewelled mitred bust, which held part of the martyr's skull, is flanked with censing angels.*

buildings serviceable for commerce survived the Dissolution.

Nearly hanged at Dover, briefly sheltered at Christchurch, five Franciscans lodged at the Poor Priests' Hospital, in September 1224, while four continued towards London and Oxford. They crept into the schoolroom at dusk, to brew a common porridge from beer lees over the embers (**50**). Their rough huts and chapel were replaced in 1267 by a popular preaching church, when John Digge acquired them land on the island of Binnewith. Only a small two-storey building of unknown purpose survives, straddling the Stour beside the riverside walk. The first Franciscan archbishop, Pecham, encouraged their sermons at Christchurch Priory and throughout the diocese. They also tended poor pilgrims at Eastbridge Hospital nearby. Their numbers averaged 35 when Edward IV made them one of six strict Observant English houses in 1498, a reform which retained their popularity to the end.

Downstream, refectory and guest hall survive on either bank at Blackfriars. About 30 Domin-icans stayed here, *en route* for London and the universities, or resting from preaching tours. They patronized the gild of parish clerks and citizens frequented their churchyard for open-air sermons, protest meetings and burials. Their aisleless church and claustral buildings have gone, but the flint refectory of 1260, with reader's pulpit, survives, on an undercroft frequently adapted against the flooding caused by St Augustine's mill downstream. Its roof, of timber donated by Henry III, retains some thirteenth-century tie-beams and octagonal crown-posts, now at the King's School Arts Centre. In the 1320s Christchurch carpenters probably built the surviving roof of the guest hall, now a community centre; it had an upstairs hearth on a stone plinth (**51**).

50 *Hearths at Poor Priests' Hospital (Heritage Museum). These are preserved under a hatch in the hall; above are original smoke-blackened beams. Despite later alterations successive open hearths continued. Fireplaces for the Elizabethan Bridewell and school are visible in the walls above later inserted floors.*

51 *A reconstruction of Blackfriars before 1538. Two western buildings survive but modern King Street runs through the eastern cloister range and chancel. The rest was quickly adapted as a cloth factory in 1538 and became the Walloons' official weaving hall. Part was the home of Dr John Peters, a successful immigrant. Seventeenth-century Baptists used the Refectory where Defoe preached.*

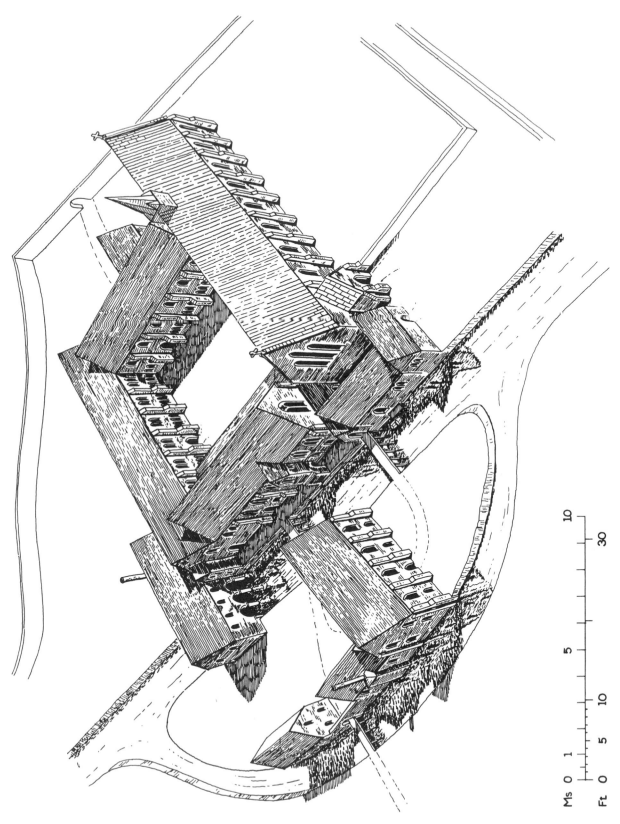

Splinter groups with penitential aims were formed among the friars in the 1250s, such as the extremist Friars of the Sack, whose community in St Peter's Street was dispersed in 1314. The site was offered to the contemplative Augustinian Whitefriars, who preferred to squat in St George's parish, paying neither tithe to the vicar nor rent to Christchurch. Quarrels resolved, 18 Whitefriars built a church and precinct 'by the cloth market', which legal patrons twice restored in the fifteenth century. This was their heyday, when their church hosted gild ceremonies and was filled with altars and chantries. Demolished at the Dissolution and bombed in 1942, only the name remains in Whitefriars shopping precinct.

City worthies

William Caudwell, founder of St Sepulchre's nunnery, was the last single portreeve, in a succession dating from 780. When two bailiffs replaced him, the Burghmote, representing the six city wards, already met on alternate Tuesdays, summoned by the eleventh-century Burghmote horn, still sounded at Mayor-making. In 1215, when other towns gained civic rights, James de Porta, the Archbishop's gatekeeper, was described as 'Maior circuitus Cantie'. Typically, he had a stone house in Palace Street, leased other tenements and represented Northgate Ward. When he died in 1216, King John forbade a replacement, Canterbury being identified with Langton's opposition to him over Magna Carta. Only in 1234 did Henry III grant the city the 'fee farm', whereby the elected bailiffs collected all Crown dues, paying £60 annually in a lump sum to the Exchequer. Partial autonomy allowed local custom to develop so that the burgess gild of Domesday Book became a formal assembly of 36, consisting of two bailiffs, six aldermen, 12 jurats and 16 councillors. This development inhibited independent craft and trade gilds; weak 'fraternities' were closely supervised by the jurats.

These 'new men', rather than the church, were founding thirteenth-century charities and patronizing the friars. Maynier the Rich had founded a hospital and chapel for seven poor citizens under Henry II which still exists in later buildings. To lodge the flood of poor, sick pilgrims sleeping rough, Edward FitzOdbold of St Peter's parish founded, about 1190, the hospice of St Thomas upon Eastbridge, under the mastership of Becket's nephew. A merchant, William Cockyn, founded the adjacent Hospital, of Saints Nicholas and Katharine, which was joined to St Thomas', with better endowments, before the Black Death. Founded for 'poor pilgrims, infirm persons, the poor and homeless and lying-in women', healthy pilgrims were limited to one night's stay at a maximum cost of 4d. The sick and pregnant had 12 beds, those dying could be buried in the Cathedral graveyard and all was to be supervised by a discreet woman 'over 40'. The surviving Transitional stone undercroft was the dormitory; the contemporary refectory above has lost two bays but retains a fine arcade with carved capitals and a thirteenth-century wall-painting of Christ in majesty. Here the Greyfriars fed the pilgrims before vespers in the chapel upstairs. Its magnificent thirteenth-century king-strut and scissor-braced roof has been recently exposed with the contemporary timberwork base of a small spire (**52**); Canterbury is fortunate in having four of these early roofs. The University bought some of the hospital's medieval lands, allowing modernization of the continuing almshouses.

Alexander of Gloucester carried out major alterations around 1220 to the 1175 stone house of the moneyer Lambin Frese, built on Priory land by the river. The chapel for his hospital for poor priests was built at right angles to the

52 *Eastbridge Hospital chapel roof. This king-strut and scissor-braced thirteenth-century roof and spirelet base are rare survivals alongside examples at St Augustine's and Christchurch. Crown-posts superseded this form of construction around 1300. The spirelet shows the carpenter's ingenuity in supporting the octagonal structure and relieving the weight on the tie-beam.*

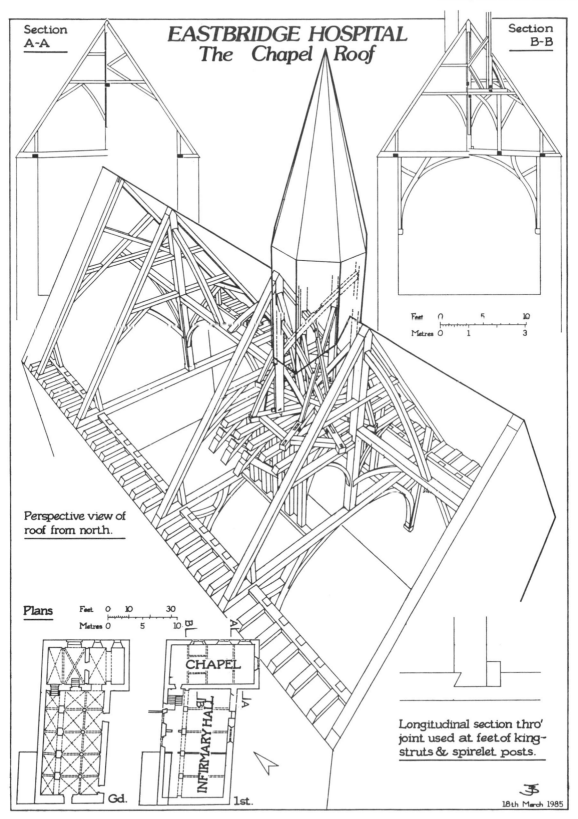

Section
A-A

EASTBRIDGE HOSPITAL
The Chapel Roof

Section
B-B

Feet 0 5 10
Metres 0 1 3

Perspective view of
roof from north.

Plans

Feet 0 10 30
Metres 0 5 10

CHAPEL

INFIRMARY HALL

Gd.

1st.

Longitudinal section thro'
joint used at feet of king-
struts & spirelet posts.

18th March 1985

75

hall, with kitchen behind. Excavation ahead of the new Heritage Museum has recovered this fine building, extensively mutilated by its post-Dissolution history as workhouse, school, museum and clinic. The smoke-blackened timbers of the museum's roof illustrate centuries of open fires on the central hearths laid bare (see **49**). In the 1370s the Master acquired a private solar and undercroft beyond a new chalk wall where he enjoyed fine tile-decorated fireplaces. The old hall gained larger windows and new kitchens beyond a screens passage shifted from north to south, but the old priests still had their open hearth in a new position.

The Black Death and after

As in other pilgrimage towns where people flocked to invoke Heaven's protection, bubonic plague hit Canterbury hard, early in 1348; three Masters of Eastbridge pilgrims' hospital died within three years. At 10,000, Canterbury's population had been in the country's top ten; by the early sixteenth century it was only 3000. Numbers dropped early, by 50 per cent, and fell further as recurrent outbreaks, up to 1440, were supplemented by tuberculosis, sweating sickness, typhoid, dysentery, pneumonia and measles. The city's fortunes fluctuated – from 1350 to 1420, despite a high death rate, it was a buoyant and exciting place. Houses were full, pilgrimage was at a peak, as chronicled in Chaucer's *Canterbury Tales*, defences were repaired and the Cathedral nave rebuilt. The period 1420–1470 was a bad one, with empty houses and falling rents, inaugurated by a five-year trade slump, but 1470–1520 saw a modest revival. Properties refilled and rents rose piecemeal. Although wealth was by then concentrated among fewer families, they were building themselves fine new timber-framed houses (see Topic: Chapter 6).

The Archaeological Trust's bone department is studying over 1300 medieval skeletons revealing that life for commoners was 'nasty, brutish and short'. Scurvy, rickets, anaemia, arthritis and bad teeth produced a life of chronic pain

and deformity for many, while infant mortality of 31 per cent may be an underestimate. Twenty-two per cent of adult females died under 30, some buried with unborn and newborn children, showing the commonest cause of death. Older skeletons show the wear and tear of working life with flattened skulls and curved spines from carrying heavy loads, healed fractures and teeth worn by chewing leather to soften it.

The religious houses cushioned Canterbury from the worst effects of decline, since demand for food and services remained strong, buttressed by a policy-switch into leasing out farmlands rather than depending on them for supplies. Abbey and Priory maintained the number and condition of their city properties, despite a 75 per cent drop in rental income and a fall in bequests; people were preferring to endow their parish churches, fraternities, specific charities or the Friars. Migrants from surrounding villages, loosed from manorial ties, came to this pilgrimage town for jobs, but the living was scanty among many small traders in clothing, textiles, leather and pottery.

The churches reflect these events. In the poor southern quarter, St Mary de Castro gained St John's congregation in 1349, while St Edmund Ridingate joined another parish. Both buildings disappeared but in 1486, St Mary's itself was amalgamated with St Mildred's, which gained a new north aisle. St Margaret's, St Peter's and St Dunstan's also built new aisles for expanded congregations. The Cathedral precinct swallowed up St Mary Queningate by 1400 and work on the city defences involved rebuilding St Michael's on Burgate and Holy Cross above Westgate alongside their old sites.

Defences

The French Wars brought an urgent review of city's defences. In 1363, a Commission of Inquiry found that the disrepair of 1100 years, stone-robbing and ditch-filling had eroded the Roman circuit. For thirty years from 1378 kings commended bailiffs for removing encroachments, ordered them to use Kentish masons and authorized five murage grants (Fr. 'mur' = wall) towards the cost. In 1380 Archbishop Sudbury gave a lead by part-financing the replacement for Westgate, supervised by the king's master mason Henry Yevele, then working on a new gatehouse at the Castle (**53**).

The gate was surveyed archaeologically in 1981. Yevele had used gunloops at Lord Cobham's Cooling Castle, near Rochester, and gave Westgate inverted keyhole gunloops on the three floors of each drum tower. Hand guns, as portable as a bag of golf-clubs, could be lifted to all floors and traversed through 45 degrees. The top floor and battlemented parapet are poorer work and may be of later date, after the interruption of the Peasants' Revolt, when Archbishop Sudbury, who had financed the gate, was murdered. Simultaneously the parish church of Holy Cross, situated above the old gate as at Northgate, was spaciously replaced alongside. In 1978 it was converted into the city Guildhall, but remains a rare Kentish example of a new fourteenth-century church.

Scars survive where Westgate joined the walls but it now stands isolated and chipped by modern traffic, its defensive impact diluted although its symbolic message remains strong. It owes its lone survival among city gates to its long use as the city gaol.

Some wall repairs occurred earlier, as in Burgate Lane where workmen had cut through a foot of soil-dumping to reach Roman masonry foundations. The Roman wall circuit with new wall towers was virtually rebuilt by 1402. Eight square towers, mostly on the northern side, and 16 open horseshoe-shaped towers have been identified; most have battered ashlar plinths and gun ports. Although some may be of late fifteenth-century date when further upgrading occurred, stratified pottery below one dates it from 1390.

Priors of Christchurch were active in these periods; Chillenden, in the 1390s, was responsible for the stretch of wall and towers from North-

gate to Queningate and Selling from thence to Burgate. By his day Roman Queningate was blocked. In the later period, attention focused on renewing Newingate and Burgate; both were excavated in 1988. Mayors contributed towards Newingate, but communal effort completed it between 1483 and 1495 with ragstone from Maidstone, flints from Downland villages delivered at 1s a cartload and £30 9s 7d collected from strangers and the city wards. It was an old-fashioned version of Westgate; its massive ashlar skirts survived its 1801 demolition below the ring road (**54**). Money was collected for Burgate in the 1470s but it was only completed in 1525, in brick and stone, with semi-octagonal towers (**55**). It still boasted gunloops, crenellations and portcullis and its flint foundations lie in the old ditch. Both gates are now outlined in the roadway.

Rebellion and civil war

Archbishop Sudbury's local benefactions are annually remembered by the Christmas mayoral procession to his tomb; Chancellor Sudbury, scapegoat for the detested Poll Tax, was the object of hatred during the revolt of 1381. In June, Wat Tyler led his following into Canterbury unopposed to sack the Castle, empty the gaol, burn the county legal and financial records and loot the Archbishop's Palace. Disrupting a service, they shouted to the monks to choose themselves a new Primate as they would soon need one. The bailiffs were not deposed, although forced to swear fealty to 'King Richard and the Commons', but were powerless to prevent the settling of old scores. Three alleged 'traitors' were dragged out and beheaded in the street; other suspects had property ransacked for inconvenient leases and bonds. East Kent recruits, arriving after the rebels had left for London, there to behead Sudbury, rampaged for several days so extensively that Canterbury was excluded from the general amnesty afterwards.

Things were different in June 1450. Jack Cade and 4000 followers, rising against Lan-

THE WESTGATE
CANTERBURY
A restored and cutaway view from the south c1400

©John Atherton Bowen 1993

53 *Westgate around 1400. Finely-coursed ragstone ashlar drum-towers with massive stone skirts jutted from the plinth into the river. A drawbridge led to a recessed entrance guarded by machicolations and portcullis. The bosses of the elegant rib-vault acted as murder-holes.*

castrian misrule, waited three hours outside Westgate before Mayor Clifton, backed by public opinion, denied them entry. He had arrested 'Blewbeard' Cheyne that January during a premature rising which attacked St Radegund's hospice, near Northgate. Afterwards, 29 city leaders wisely obtained pardons to secure immunity from prosecution, among them gentlemen, past and future mayors and MPs and wine, paper and livestock merchants. Canterbury witnessed hangings in 1451 during punitive sessions dubbed 'the harvest of heads'.

The difference between 1381 and 1451 may lie partly in the benefits of Lancastrian favour, culminating in the City Charter of 1448. Henry

IV, a munificent patron of the Cathedral, is the only sovereign buried there; Archbishop Chichele and the choirboys welcomed Henry V there after Agincourt and Henry VI was a frequent pilgrim. The Charter gave Canterbury a mayor and one of the elected bailiffs executed the legal and financial offices of the high sheriff in the city. In 1461 Canterbury was to be a County 'for ever', a status lasting until 1974; the city still has a Lord Mayor and Sheriff.

Mayors chose sides less wisely under the Yorkists. Edward IV had Mayor Faunt hanged

54 *St George's Gate foundations in 1988. Roman wall and rampart material underlay the greensand 'Newingate' which spanned a carriageway 2.1m (7ft) wide. No datable finds emerged to establish the chronology more closely than c. tenth century. Ironworks occupied its crumbling ditch by 1483–95, when this replacement, modelled on Westgate, was built. Battered skirts of ragstone ashlar appeared below the ring road. It was demolished in 1801.*

55 *Burgate in the sixteenth century. Traces of Burgate's Roman predecessor leading to Richborough survived. Layers of street metalling proved its importance for the Saxon inner burgh until superseded by Newingate. It was rebuilt in 1525, possibly to Robert Vertue's design, and converted into a dwelling which lasted until 1781.*

in the Buttermarket in 1471 for aiding the Fauconbridge rising; the same week Mayor Clifton, hero of 1450, was executed by Yorkists following the battle of Tewkesbury. The Cathedral did better, attracting continuous patronage from Richard II, the Lancastrian kings and Edward IV in turn for rebuilding the nave and transepts. In a final flourish under Henry VII, Cardinal Morton financed Bell Harry Tower (**56**). Christchurch Gate was built by Prior Goldstone II, whose canting coat of arms surmounts its smaller arch. Building and transport trades benefited from these works and the great inns (see Topic) all going up between 1381 and 1517.

Although incomers and artisans might respond to the turbulence of rebellion or Lollardy, city government came under the control of a close-knit group of local gentry, merchants and lawyers who were buying a portfolio of properties for city revenue. City pride revived in the 1480s. Accounts show payments for setting the city arms in the Guildhall windows, for buying blue and silver uniforms for the city band or repairing and cleaning streets, regulating markets and especially for financing St Thomas' Marching Watch. This annual day-long re-enactment of the Murder on a pageant cart was accompanied by band, watch and fraternity processions with banners and floats. A boy played Becket for 3s 4d; the Knights had 2d and free beer, while a child, crouched behind the altar, squirted pig's blood on the saint and operated an angel's wings as his soul ascended to heaven. St Dunstan's parish and the Gild of Corpus Christi each performed summer plays near Westgate. Perhaps these innovations aimed to boost business when shrine receipts had dropped to under £50 per annum. Certainly a sense of civic identity would

be vital in the next century when Canterbury's great religious houses, its world-famous shrine and its old *raison d'être* were to vanish.

Topic: Pilgrim Inns

In the fifteenth century, Christchurch Priory led the way in providing pilgrim inns, taverns and lodging houses in the city, responding belatedly to a demand already shrinking (see **colour plate 9**). These supplemented the hospices for the poor and sick like St Thomas, Eastbridge, and the monastic guesthouses and almonries throughout the Cathedral precincts and at the outer court of St Augustine's Abbey.

56 *Canterbury Cathedral from the south-east. John Wastell's Bell Harry tower, completed in 1504, crowned 400 years of building. The Romanesque chapels of St Anselm's day, surviving the fire of 1174, clasp the French Gothic choir of William of Sens. Henry Yevele's Perpendicular nave, within Lanfranc's dimensions, lies beyond. The full length is flanked by Mapilton's south-west tower of 1423–33 and the thirteenth-century corona of William the Englishman is best appreciated in **78**.*

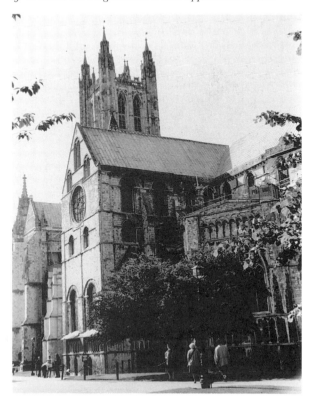

The famous Cheker of the Hope, on the west corner of Mercery Lane, was the setting for 'The Tale of Beryn', the continuation of the *Canterbury Tales* (**57**). Built by Christchurch Priory over three years from 1392, towards the end of Chaucer's lifetime, it cost £867 14s 4d. Most of the eastern side survived a fire in 1865 which destroyed two-thirds of the building. Three windows found recently, with traces of gold paint and fire-scorching, were part of the first-floor gallery overlooking the internal courtyard (**58**). From Mercery Lane can be viewed the stone arcade of its groundfloor shops, the gratings for its extensive cellars, its magnificent roofs and two of its original traceried windows. An inventory of 1533 details

rooms such as 'The White Hart' and 'St George's Chamber'. Down the Lane towards the Cathedral stood The Crown, containing 'The Sandwych Chamber'. Its vaulted cellars survive as Debenham's restaurant.

To the east of Christchurch Gate stood The Sun tavern (now Pizzaland), also built by the Priory in 1437; its tenants are continuously documented to 1661. Many of its massive timbers are exposed in the Cathedral Gate Hotel, occupying its upper part. The eastern end (now Cornell's), despite rebuilding, retains its vaulted cellar, two original windows below the tilehanging, and a unique twin crown-plate roof. It faced the Bullstake (now Buttermarket), where animals were once baited, in the belief that the joints would be more tender. Here, in 1466, John Coppyn of Whitstable and John Bigg of Canterbury erected a market cross, praying for 'God's solace in Heaven', to the horror of a Puritan mayor who removed it in 1645, coining farthings from its lead roof.

57 *'Cheker' Inn. As at the earlier 'Bull', Prior Chillenden's huge 'Cheker' inn was multi-purpose. Although fire destroyed two-thirds of it in 1865, shop refurbishment allows building recorders to reveal surviving detail from earlier cellars and the extent of the stone arcaded ground floor, to crown-post roof.*

58 *'Cheker' Inn: a window detail. Work at two Mercery Lane shops discovered part of the continuous range of second-floor gallery windows and a similar range below with different tracery. Doorways to other courtyard ranges and complicated roof carpentry at the angle of High Street and Mercery Lane survived.*

Prior Goldstone I (1449–68) replaced the 'great stone house' of The White Bull, which stood from before 1200 opposite the old cemetery gate. Its stone cellars survive below Cranfield's Camera Shop, in the middle of the double-jettied range on Burgate of Goldstone's Bull Inn, described as 'a wooden building of many lodgings' (**59**). The grandest apartments, with fireplaces, were in the double-jettied range facing the Bullstake. Shops have always occupied the ground floor (now Talisman and Laura Ashley). Access to the lodgings above was by separate staircases, as at Oxford or Cambridge colleges or the Inns of Court. The least desirable apartments adjoined the Shambles, in the single-jettied range on Butch-

ery Lane; the remains of the old courtyard opens off this lane. Liberty's, collaborating with the Archaeological Trust, sensitively restored this corner and replaced its dragon-post. It now reveals its original door and window arrangement.

Burgate's other inns, including The Porpoise, The Dolphin and The Mitre, were leased from the Priory, but yet more existed elsewhere. The Red Lion stood east of the Guildhall and was bought by the City Council in 1408, who rebuilt it 'with several considerable alterations'. It was the community's talking-shop until it disappeared when Guildhall Street was cut in 1806; the Guildhall itself was regrettably demolished in 1950. Adjoining The Red Lion was another late medieval shop with accommodation above (now Dewhursts) which has recently suffered heavily in a fire, a perennial Canterbury hazard.

The corner of 8/9 The Parade and 25/26 St Margaret's Street is another double-jettied, L-shaped group of late medieval lodgings with

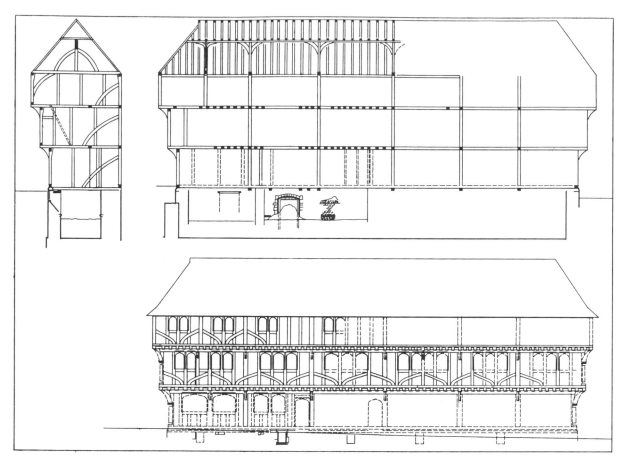

59 *'White Bull' Inn: Burgate elevation. Work for Liberty's at the left end of this building enabled this drawing to reveal the huge size and triple function of the inn, with shops, apartments and dormitories occupying successive floors. It measures 29.4m (96$\frac{1}{2}$ft) overall. Liberty's sensitive conversion largely restored its original appearance from the street.*

shops below. These inns were set round with churches and markets. St Andrew's constricted the street in the Parade. St Mary 'Bredman' beside the bread market faced the Cheker. The Rush market, beyond Butter Market, occupied modern Sun Street and a row of timber-framed shops stood just inside Christchurch Gate, where the Michaelmas Fair was held. A walk from 'The Canterbury Tales' experience to Christchurch Gate, while mentally removing later bays, windows and shop fascias, provides some impression of the vast scale of fifteenth-century tourist developments in relation to the surrounding street scene. The curious visitor, contemplating the scale of the 1992 Longmarket scheme may reflect that nothing changes (see **81**).

6

Destroyers and improvers

Between the Reformation and the Railway Age, Canterbury recovered from the loss of its shrine and monasteries by remaining the focus of East Kent, still hosting great events and welcoming Protestant refugees with new skills. Its past cast a long shadow, impelling equally the Whitefriar John Stone and the Protestant martyrs to die heroically; the antiquarian, Somner, a century later, to preserve its heritage and the banker, Simmons, in his day, to revive and modernize it. The confidence which launched the world's first passenger railway service in May 1830 would have surprised Lambarde, in 1576:

> Canterbury is in these days become in a manner waste, seeing God in all ages hath not spared to extend his vengeance upon the places where his name was dishonoured. viz., Sodom, Jerusalem and others. So Canterbury came suddenly from great wealth and multitudes of beautiful buildings to extreme poverty, nakedness and decay...in which plight for pity I leave it.

The Dissolution of the Monasteries

The monks attending Henry VIII, Wolsey and the Emperor Charles V to Becket's shrine in 1520, could hardly foresee the relentless destruction of the next twenty years. Piecemeal suppression had begun in Kent when, in 1534, two Christchurch monks and two Greyfriars were hanged at Tyburn for treason, implicated with Canterbury's Benedictine nun, Elizabeth Barton, who had prophesied against Henry's marriage to Anne Boleyn. Margaret Roper brought the head of her executed father, Sir Thomas More, to St Dunstan's church in 1535 (**60**). St Gregory's Priory, St Sepulchre's nunnery and the three friaries were closed between 1536 and 1538 and St Augustine's Abbey surrendered itself. Meanwhile, trumpeting for 30 days at the shrine, a herald pursuivant summoned Becket to face treason charges in London. In his 'absence', the Attorney-General declared 'his goods' forfeit, so when the shrine was demolished, 4994oz of gold and 5286oz of silver, 'besides jewels of which no record remains', were among the treasures removed to the Tower. 'Bishop Becket's' images, pictures, name and feasts were obliterated throughout the kingdom. Anne of Cleves had already lodged in the refurbished Palace at St Augustine's before Cranmer surrendered Christchurch Priory in March 1540. Twenty-three monks were pensioned, including Prior Goldwell, with £80 a year, who lived on to 1555, protesting 'I will never desire to forsake my habit, religious men having continued in this our church these nine hundred years'. In 1541 half of the 12 prebends of the New Foundation of Dean and Chapter were ex-monks; 28 in all were re-employed, comparing badly with other cathedrals, since Cranmer said of them 'they are neither good teachers, nor good learners but good vianders'. He wanted

60 *The Roper Chantry Chapel, St Dunstan's Church, c. 1524. The chapel contains the tombs of this legal family who flourished from the fifteenth century and included William, son-in-law and first biographer of Sir Thomas More. They lost wealth and status by continuing as Roman Catholics. Surveyed in 1978, the vault's contents were so jumbled that the supposed skull of More, in a lead box, is conjectural, although an object of modern pilgrimage.*

20 learned divines and 40 university students under the new regime but only got six itinerant preachers and a local school of 50 boys with two teachers in an establishment of 135, including also a choral foundation and minor canons. Refectory and Dormitory were demolished but other precinct buildings were adapted for the prebends' houses (**61**). Archaeological surveys at five dissolved establishments have recently been possible.

The aftermath

From 1537, anti-clerical Protestant radicals controlled the city council; they fomented image-breaking, suppressed St Thomas' Marching Watch and backed a Protestant printing press. When St Augustine's was surrendered they acquired 98 houses and Abbot's Mill for the city. Humbler citizens bought stone at 8d a cartload or acquired auctioned spoons or chairs which appeared in later inventories.

Church and cloister at this fourteenth richest abbey in England, worth £1733 per annum, were systematically levelled by James Needham, the king's agent. Stone and lead went to Calais' defences or to new castles near Deal; the rest was hastily converted into a royal staging-post on the Dover road (**62**). Thirty-

61 *New Foundation after 1541. This map, based on Hill's 1680 plan, published in Battley's* Cantuaria Sacra *(1703), incorporates Willis' findings in the 1860s. New houses within the walls of unroofed claustral buildings augmented quarters adapted for legal, financial, scholastic and domestic use. Temporarily subdivided under the Commonwealth, they suffered less than the Archbishop's Palace. (Taken from a full precinct survey by CAT.)*

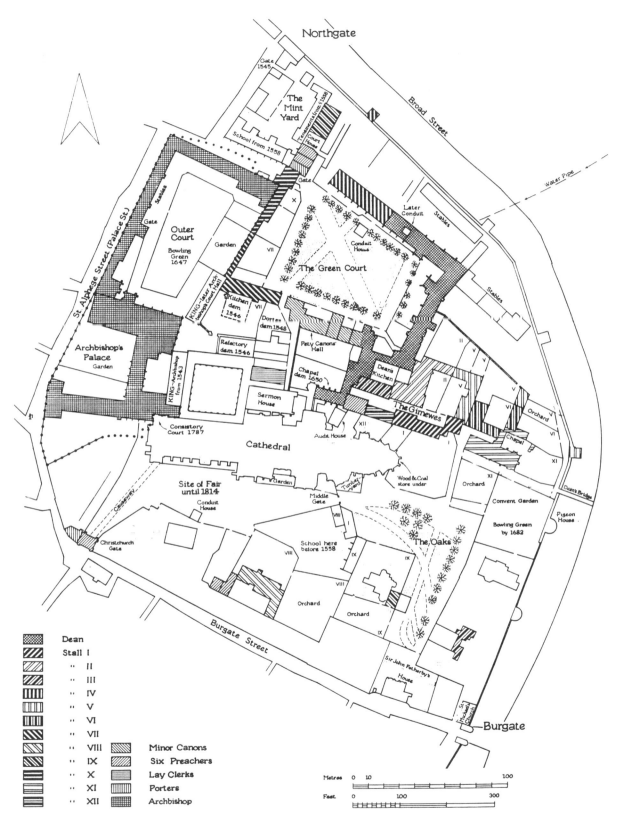

Northgate

Gate 1545

The Mint Yard

Tenements from 1558

School from 1558

Court House

Broad Street

Water Pipe

Gate

Stables

X

Later Conduit

Stables

St Alphege Street (Palace St.)

Gate

Outer Court

Bowling Green 1647

Garden

VII

Conduit House

The Green Court

KING-later Arch. bishops Court Hall

Kitchen dem 1546

VII

Dortes dem 1548

Petty Canons' Hall

Stables

Archbishop's Palace

Garden

KING-Archbishop from 1543

Refectory dem 1546

Chapel dem 1650

Dean's Kitchen

II

V

V

V

Orchard

II

Sermon House

The Gimewes

I

Chapel

XII

VI

Consistory Court 1787

Audit House

I

XI

Cathedral

Garden

Tunbist Yard

Wood & Coal store under

XI

Orchard

Dean's Bridge

Site of Fair until 1814

Conduit House

Middle Gate

VIII

Convent Garden

Pigeon House

Christchurch Gate

School here before 1558

VIII

I

IX

IX

The Oaks

Bowling Green by 1682

VIII

Orchard

Orchard

IX

Burgate Street

Sir John Fotherby's House

St Michaels Church

Burgate

▨	Dean
▨	Stall I
▨	" II
▨	" III
▥	" IV
▥	" V
▥	" VI
▨	" VII
▨	" VIII
▨	" IX
▤	" X
▤	" XI
▤	" XII

Minor Canons

Six Preachers

Lay Clerks

Porters

Archbishop

Metres 0 10   100

Feet 0   100   300

one monks were pensioned, but only 200 out of their 2000 priceless manuscripts survive today and one item from the treasury. The home farm quickly passed through several local lessees, before staying with an Elizabethan financier, Sir Thomas Smythe.

Although claustral buildings were made uninhabitable lest 'the birds should nest again', good houses and industrial buildings survived. When the prior and six canons, accused of all-night dicing parties, left St Gregory's, it was worth £166 4s 5½d. It soon reverted from Crown to Archbishop, who supervised the continuing St John's Hospital and cemetery but leased the prior's lodging to a lawyer who retained guardianship of the archbishop's archives. His son, Thomas Neville, became Dean of Canterbury and benefactor of Trinity College, Cambridge.

The Observant Greyfriars, after their warden's execution, endured house arrest for their last four years. The property came to the poet Lovelace's family. The prior of Blackfriars prudently fled abroad, after preaching against Henry's breach with Rome. Blackfriars became a weaving factory a year after Richard Ingworth, Bishop of Dover, once the Order's English head, dissolved both friaries on 13 December 1538.

Ingworth met his match at Whitefriars a day later. John Stone 'rudely and traiterously used us before all the company', as he reported to Thomas Cromwell, 'at all times he still held and wills to die for it, that the King may not be the head of the Church of England but it must be a spiritual father, appointed by God.' After a year's imprisonment in London and Canterbury, Stone died barbarously in December 1539. Dragged on a hurdle to Dane John, he was part hanged, his heart cut out alive and his members parboiled to be put on the gates. City accounts survive recording payments of 2d to the woman scouring the kettle and 2d for 'a lamb to Mr Mayor when the justices did sit'.

62 *St Augustine's Royal Palace, 1539. Three hundred men worked round the clock to complete a new south range and adapt others in the Great Court for Anne of Cleves, who stayed one night. Leased to royal courtiers, like Lord Wootton, who had John Tradescant Senior lay out the grounds, royalty occasionally used it, such as Charles I, honeymooning in 1625.*

The Protestant martyrs

The Protestant council leaders, patronised by Cranmer, prospered under Edward, but made their peace with Mary and Philip who visited Canterbury twice. St Andrew's parish sold its lectern and restored its rood screen with a council grant; the Marching Watch was revived.

Under the Catholic reaction, 68 Kentish clergy lost their livings, mostly for marrying. When some fled abroad the survivors were leaderless so Archdeacon Harpsfield and Bishop Thornden of Dover determined to make a first public example of John Bland, outspoken Vicar of Adisham. He was burnt praying alongside another vicar and two others in a single fire in 1555. The sounds and smells must have reached Archbishop Cranmer, who played bowls in the Deanery garden while under house arrest – his own fate in the fire at Oxford lay ahead.

Forty-two people, including ten women, were burnt in this place of their trial, and five died in Canterbury Castle, the largest totals outside London. None were locals; most were humble folk from Ashford, Hythe or the Weald, areas long associated with Lollardy. As many were hanged for petty theft in 1590–3 as died for religion in 1555–8, but Canterbury's martyrs became household names after 1570, when Foxe's *Book of Martyrs* was placed beside the Bishops' Bible in every cathedral. This scrupulously researched best-seller brought back to life Alice Benden of Staplehurst, incarcerated for nine weeks in the 'Monday hole', a dark underground vault in the precincts. Lame and filthy, she came before the Bishop, who ordered a bath which completely removed her skin; she

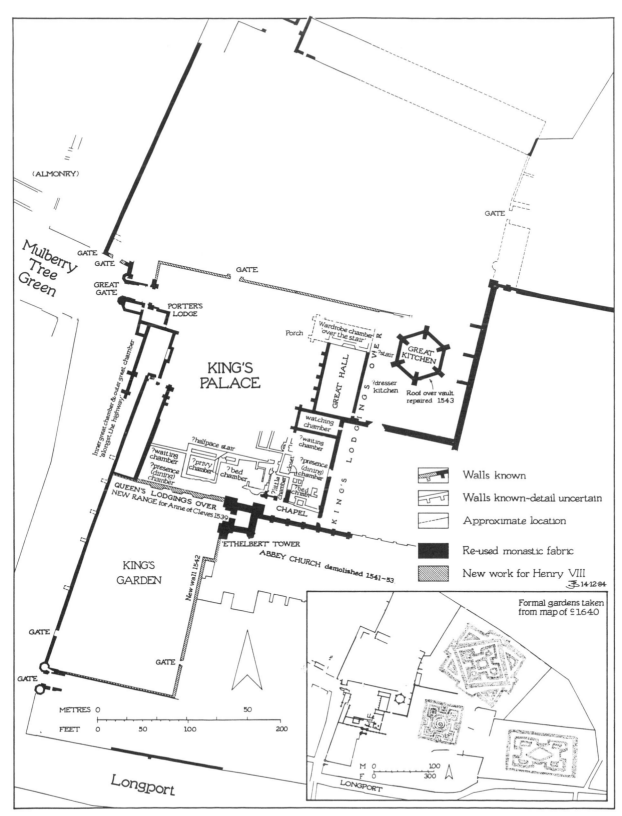

(ALMONRY)

Mulberry
Tree
Green

GATE

GATE

GATE

GREAT
GATE

PORTER'S
LODGE

Inner great chamber & outer great chamber
alongside the highway

KING'S
PALACE

Porch

Wardrobe chamber
over the stair

?stair

GREAT
KITCHEN

?dresser
kitchen

Roof over vault
repaired 1543

GREAT HALL

KING'S LODGINGS OVER

watching
chamber

?halfpace stair

?waiting
chamber

?waiting
chamber

?privy
chamber

?presence
(dining)
chamber

?bed
chamber

?presence
(dining)
chamber

?little
chamber

closet

?bed
chamber

QUEEN'S LODGINGS OVER
NEW RANGE for Anne of Cleves 1539

CHAPEL

KING'S
GARDEN

'ETHELBERT' TOWER

New wall 1542

ABBEY CHURCH demolished 1541~53

GATE

GATE

GATE

Walls known

Walls known–detail uncertain

Approximate location

Re-used monastic fabric

New work for Henry VIII

14·12·84

Formal gardens taken
from map of c.1640

METRES 0 50

FEET 0 .... 50 .... 100 200

Longport

M 0 100
F 0 300

LONGPORT

89

still refused to recant. Foxe recorded the letter of those dying in the Castle:

> We, poor prisoners for God's Truth...lie in cold irons and our keeper will not suffer any meat to be brought to comfort us. We write not to the intent we might not be famished for the Lord Jesus' sake – but they have no Law so to famish us in prison and should not do it privily.

Storms, dearth and 'flu, with vagrant soldiers from captured Calais roaming the streets, were the setting for the last burnings, only two days before the queen's own death. The Martyrs' Field monument, off Wincheap, is undeservedly neglected. The area remained waste land within living memory, where charred wood and bones were occasionally found.

Christopher Marlowe's community

The dramatist's Canterbury boyhood from 1564, reflected in his work, illuminates an exciting Elizabethan town of sharp contrasts, in a time of economic recovery, religious stability and peace. His parents, incomers from Ospringe and Dover, typify the range of inward migration which increased the population despite epidemics. His orphaned cousin, Dorothy, joined the Marlowes when her father, Westgate's gaol-keeper, died of plague. St George's parish was particularly noisy and dirty, lying between Cattlemarket and Shambles. Through its Newingate passed discharged soldiers, felons going to the nearby gallows, the Polish prince John Casimir meeting Sir Philip Sidney, and the Queen herself, celebrating her fortieth birthday. Adequate clergy were hard to find; the Revd William Sweeting, ex-tailor and parish clerk, felt incapable of delivering four sermons annually and, even with another curacy, left his family so destitute that they were lodged after his death above Newingate itself. Marlowe's quarrelsome father, minor office-holder in parish and shoemakers' gild, moved frequently in a town of social and ethnic diversity. Neighbours included 'Sir' John Dygon, late monk of St Augustine's; immigrants, like Harmon Verson, glazier; three aldermen and 'capper' Roos and his wife, the parish midwife; while Mother Bassocke begged at the door. Contemporaries of the dramatist included Stephen Gosson, polemical opponent of theatres, and John Lyly, author of *Euphues*, whose father, Registrar of the Consistory Court, was one of many lawyers. Typical was Robert Railton, the Town Clerk, a rising position as government burdens and litigation increased, who was also attorney in most of East Kent's courts.

The almshouses of two controversial lawyers survive. Sir Roger Manwood crowned a lucrative legal career by receiving the suburban royal manor of Hackington. He built brick cottages for six almspeople and the parish clerk, raised the vicar's stipend and planned a workhouse. On his death-bed, under house arrest on corruption charges, he was offering Lord Burghley bribes to become Chief Justice. His splendid monument (**63**) adorns the church where he ordered an annual sermon on 'the frailty and vain delights of this world'.

Sir John Boys MP, Canterbury's first Recorder and High Steward to five archbishops, founded Jesus Hospital in 1599 for up to 20 almspeople, near his home at old St Gregory's. By his death, his trustees had an annual income of £100. His statutes ordained that 20 poor boys 'be trained up in labour and made apt members of the Commonwealth' by the Warden, until fit for apprenticeship. A 1560s' census showed under-18s forming 45 per cent of inhabitants in poor parishes.

Cranmer, too, had ensured that the King's School became part of the New Foundation, saying 'poor men's children are many times endued with more singular gifts of nature ...and more commonly given to apply them to study than is the gentleman's son'. The 50 scholars received free meals, a gown and £1 8s 4d per annum, during four to five years' schooling. From 1573 the school occupied the old Almonry Chapel in the Mint Yard, the

63 *Sir Roger Manwood 1525–92: St Stephen's, Hackington. Colt, the immigrant sculptor of this monument, also designed Elizabeth I's at Westminster. The portrait bust, significantly clutching a money-bag, is surrounded by his family and a wooden skeleton. Manwood's own inscriptions, include 'unexpected Death snatches away a splendid life. Before, I was a Judge; now I am before the Tribunal'.*

headmaster lodging boarders in the chaplain's house. An excavation in 1979 revealed the schoolroom, containing marbles and pipes, above the thirteenth-century chapel, itself overlying a Roman road where Saxon beads were found.

Marlowe was a scholar from 1578 to 1580. His days ran from prayers at 6a.m. to prep. at 7p.m., broken by 80 compulsory Cathedral services a year and recreation, 'but whatever they play, they shall never use any language but Latin or Greek'. His Headmaster's library of 350 books included Chaucer, *Utopia* and Petrarch, alongside Latin and Greek classics and religious texts. Schoolmates were part boarder-gentry and, increasingly, short-stay artisan dayboys. Future careers ranged from Benedictine missionary to Congregationalist founder of a Virginian settlement. Many, like Marlowe, and later, William Harvey, went with one of Archbishop Parker's scholarships to Cambridge.

Scholars delivered Latin orations in 1574 when Parker royally entertained Elizabeth in his refurbished Hall. Three days of fifteen-course banquets and a ball cost him £2000. This hall, at 61m by 19.5m (200ft by 64ft) second only in size to Westminster, was built after 1200 by Hubert Walter and Stephen Langton in French Gothic style. Although demolished in 1647, small excavations and surviving fragments enabled a reconstruction to revive its splendours (**64**).

The quick-tempered, well-schooled adolescent, probably irked by small-town convention but his sensibilities aroused by its magnificence and brutality, left to live dangerously in a brief, meteoric career. A new verse form for six plays of startling poetry and passion was filling the Rose theatre by 1593. Christopher, like his father, picked local quarrels; doubtless fellow-citizens were unsurprised to learn of his violent death in suspicious circumstances. Fourth centenary celebrations in 1993 restored his memorial outside today's Marlowe Theatre. In modern Canterbury, his name is as ubiquitous as Chaucer's, even if neither is as read as he deserves.

The strangers

Persecution and war in the Spanish Netherlands brought fairly easily absorbed waves of French-speaking protestant Walloons to transform Canterbury between 1567 and 1700. The last influx of French Huguenots, however, soon migrated to Spitalfields. The Council welcomed 'profitable and gentle strangers' of sober

64 *Archbishop's Palace and Precinct in 1573. Parts of the porch and kitchen shown here survive within current buildings. Parliament ordered the hall's removal after Laud's execution. Prebendal houses are shown in Lanfranc's unroofed dormitory, but his hall, abutting the Cathedral, was incorporated in the new palace of 1899 when archbishops resumed regular residence (see **46**).*

behaviour, caring for their own poor, renting empty property and bringing new skills to the local unemployed.

They retained their home links and absorbed second-time migrants from Holland or Calais. The pastor of Armentières brought his entire flock in 1571, as did Pastor Hamon from Rye, promising to introduce 'Florence serges, Bombazines, Orleans silks, Bayes and Moquettes'. One successful immigrant, Jean-Baptiste de le Pierre (sic), was baptized a Catholic in Flanders, married by Calvinist rites in France, but was buried an Anglican, in 1689, as Dr John Peters MD, owner of Blackfriars; a descendant

lives here still. The city admitted 100 families from overcrowded Sandwich in 1576 to whom Parker gave the western crypt for their worship and school; a weekly French service is still held in the Huguenot chapel.

At first unable to own property, several families crowded each tenement in the riverside parishes, especially around Blackfriars (**65**). The Refectory became the Weavers' Hall and Market, selling cloths from 400 looms through Dover and London by 1580. Employing one native to every two strangers, the council approved 'a poor and painful people'. By the 1600s Walloons numbered about 2000 in a population of 5000; bread-rioters in the 1630s complained 'living five to six in one tenement...they take money when Englishmen cannot'. Archbishop Laud's tactless attempt to drive them into Anglican parishes, which would then have to support their poor, swung opinion their way again.

Accredited immigrants owned 'mereaux' or communion cards, confiscation of which denied them benefits. The Minister and Elders appointed deacons from each city quarter, who collected poor rates or made exceptional single payments. Obligatory services, catechism and French teaching brought people together regularly. Their Consistory Court records only one irregular pregnancy; living so congestedly, 'carnal knowledge' quickly led to shotgun weddings. Drunkenness and brawls were common when men stayed late at taverns outside Westgate or skipped afternoon service to drink at country inns. Mayoral arrest was the ultimate penalty neither side wished to invoke.

From 1676, silk weaving outstripped wool. A thousand looms employed 2700 natives and strangers, making 'Alamodes, Lustrings, Paduasoys, watered Tabbies and Estamines', admired by Celia Fiennes. Assimilation through naturalization and marrying-out began before 1685 when 1500 French arrived, 'the greater part poor, aged and other infirm and sickly persons', as the Elders complained. Many followed the enterprising Dutoits and Lemans, prospering as brocade designers in London; Canterbury relatives begin to appear in parish registers with anglicized names, like Bawdry, Ridout and Terry. Some rose from Freeman to Alderman in other trades, but weavers stayed poor, for imported Indian muslins killed local silk weaving by 1820. A microcosm of Walloon life appeared at 4–5 Best Lane (see Topic).

Pilgrims and puritans, 1620–80

Puritanism grew among lower tradesmen excluded from the council oligarchy. Robert Cushman, grocer's assistant, punished by the Church courts for Puritan fly-posting and missing church, fled to Leyden. As a respected member of that community, he was commissioned to return to Canterbury to negotiate the hire of the *Mayflower*, on which sailed James Chilton, an argumentative tailor from St Paul's parish; he signed the Mayflower Compact. Among Churchill's and Roosevelt's ancestors

65 *The 'Weavers'. The city, especially in Palace Street and Northgate, has survivors of timber-framed buildings, adapted in the seventeenth century for the looms of the Walloon weavers. One still operated until recently in this famous example on King's Bridge. The river was needed for finishing cloth. Fulling mills were later adapted for paper-making.*

were Canterbury-born Hester Mayhieu and Philippe de la Noye, who had relations here.

Laud's high-church innovations provoked some sympathy for iconoclasts. In 1642, Colonel Sandys' troop, securing Kentish arsenals for Parliament, vandalized the Cathedral and attacked Christ's statue in Christchurch Gate. Lighting their pipes from torn service books, they discharged '40 shot at least, triumphing when they did hit it . . . as if they would crucify Him again'. A 350-year gap was filled, in 1991, by Klaus Ringwald's Christ statue. A Puritan minister, 'Blue Dick' Culmer, wrought three days' havoc, with Parliamentary sanction, in 1643. A largely hostile crowd, restrained by troops, watched him using Somner's new *Antiquities of Canterbury* as 'guide to sail by in that Cathedral ocean of images' and 'rattling down proud Becket's glassy bones' from the windows.

Dissenting conventicles mushroomed under the Commonwealth when independent divines preached in the Cathedral and the old Chapter House, known as the Sermon House. Baptists were established at Blackfriars before the Restoration. Flourishing Congregationalists followed their minister Durant, a washball maker, to St Paul's parish, when he was ejected from the Sermon House in 1662. Quakers were organizing East Kent within 14 years of their arrival in 1654 and Presbyterians acquired Greyfriars in the 1670s.

Royalist reaction, 1647–80

Old loyalties surfaced on Christmas Day 1647, when the Puritan Mayor banned services and ordered a Precincts Fair. He was assaulted, stalls overturned, prisons emptied and free drink enjoyed by footballers in the High Street. When the city declared for 'God, King Charles and Kent', the County Trained Bands arrived to force capitulation; gates were burned, the city wall near the Castle slighted and guns trained inwards, before packed juries tried the rioters in April 1648. Their refusal to convict kindled the rising of Kentish gentry which became the second civil war. Following his bloody victory at Maidstone, Fairfax secured Canterbury's peaceful capitulation, combatants surrendering 3000 weapons and 300 horses at the Cathedral. East Kent was now a high-risk area, strictly controlled, especially under Major-General Kelsey.

The Archbishop's Palace was pillaged or demolished and Prebends' houses let as tenements, although Thomas Monins, the sequestrator, strove to finance repairs while paying choir, King's Scholars and St John's almsfolk. William Somner discovered and hid the Jaco-

bean font, returning it for his own daughter's baptism in 1660, when his Auditor's report lamented that 'whatever was money-worth was made prize of and embezzled', especially priceless library books and records.

Battered Canterbury joyfully welcomed Charles II on 22 May 1660. The scarlet-robed Corporation presented a gold tankard, while Somner gave the King his own sumptuously bound book. Processing from St Augustine's Palace to the Cathedral through garlanded streets, Charles deplored the dilapidations, but commented that the people seemed glad to hear the Common Prayer again. Archbishop Juxon could restore the Cathedral gate and order magnificent choir stalls but found staffing his parishes as hard as Cranmer and Parker before him. A survey of 1682 found 'a good, honest poor man of 80' at St Dunstan's; a 'bragging talker, dissolute and much in debt' at All Saints, while sectaries and schismatics 'infested' St Andrew's, St Mildred's and St Paul's.

Eighteenth-century revival

By 1830 perhaps fifty, or half, the dominant families in a town of 14,000, actively sought the power and prestige of civic office. To them, modernization meant the destruction of outdated medieval constrictions, to improve streets and cut new ones for the fashionable coaching trade. Thus, the 'Nobles, Gentry and Retired Persons' of Stapleton's Directory would be drawn to give 'Tone and Trade to the Town'. The Freeman borough returned two MPs; close alliances developed during three-day polls at open hustings, when houses bulged with Freeman relatives returning to vote.

The coaching trade

All main routes were turnpiked by 1800. Six coaches from three principal inns, supplemented by Royal and Foreign Mail coaches, ran 91 weekly journeys (see **colour plate 10**). For 18 shillings you could reach London in six hours or connect with sailing hoys and steamboats. Combined tickets took you by channel packet to Paris for three guineas. Eight hotels, 69 taverns and eight eating houses were major employers. The 'Falstaff Tap' survives to show how servants and ostlers were segregated behind inn yards.

Coaches like cars engineered change. From 1787, the Commissioners of Paving, Lighting and Watching ordered 'all projections, port-icoes, pediments, signs, steps and rails whatever' to encroach no more than 12 inches on the street. All gates, save Westgate, the city gaol, were demolished, thereby removing St Mary Northgate's chancel. St Margaret's chancel went to enable coaches to swing into the 'Fountain' opposite. St Andrew's and Middle Row disappeared from the Parade. All Saints lost its tower and was later rebuilt further back, when dismantling King's Mill enabled the bottleneck at Eastbridge to be widened with stones from demolished stretches of north-western city wall. New Guildhall Street gave access to the Margate Road.

Market town

A varied hinterland made Canterbury East Kent's market. All-year employment for whole families depended on 6000 acres (2428 ha) of local hopgrounds; 313 new Freemen rep-resented brewing interests. The old-established cattle and butter markets were joined by the elegant Corn and Hop Exchange (**66**) and the Greek-porticoed fish market. The Michaelmas Jack and Joan Hiring Fair provided several days' holiday in the precincts. Smeaton dra-matically altered the city skyline, in 1792, with Denne's Mill, 100ft high, where 250 quarters of flour were processed weekly on 16 working floors; it burnt down in 1934. It occupied the site of old Abbot's Mill, while paper was produced at the old Christchurch Barton Mill. The first Williamson arrived from Fife in 1780 to make leather. Parliaments worldwide use Canterbury leather from the tannery still man-aged by Williamsons.

A great entrepreneur, Alderman James Sim-

mons, realized that heavy goods needed better transport to London markets and dreamed of 100 ton ships below Canterbury's walls. He proposed canalizing the Stour to Sandwich and, when he died as MP in 1807, his associates backed two further canal schemes and eventu-ally the Whitstable railway. Born and educated in the city, he became joint proprietor of the Canterbury Bank (now Lloyd's). As printer and bookseller, he founded the continuing *Kentish Gazette*, in 1768. Financer of Guildhall Street, dynamo of the Paving Commissioners, benefactor of hospital and public gardens he created more than he destroyed.

The regiments

An improved town, amply provided, at the centre of a modern road network attracted the army during the French wars. From 1794 to 1811 cavalry, infantry and artillery barracks housing 5000 troops were constructed to the north, along the line of the old priory water system, which they utilized. Modern estates have obliterated most of the barracks and family housing, but Regency St Dunstan's Terrace, built for officers, still shows how mews and batmen's houses developed in New Street behind.

Social capital

Officers enjoyed amenities already patronized by gentry such as Edward Knight and his sister Jane Austen. Simmons, from 1790, landscaped the Dane John mound (**67**), now bearing his memorial obelisk, and laid out the walks and lime avenue where military bands played. St Augustine's brewery gardens staged fireworks, acrobatics and balloon ascents, while the Aug-ust Race meeting and February theatre season punctuated the year. Circulating libraries, Assembly Rooms, a Catch Club and dancing school supplemented the serious attractions of the Philosophical Institution of 1769, housing a 2000-volume library, lecture hall and museum, the nucleus of the present city collec-tions. One winter, lectures comprised 'The Philosophy of the Mind', 'The History of

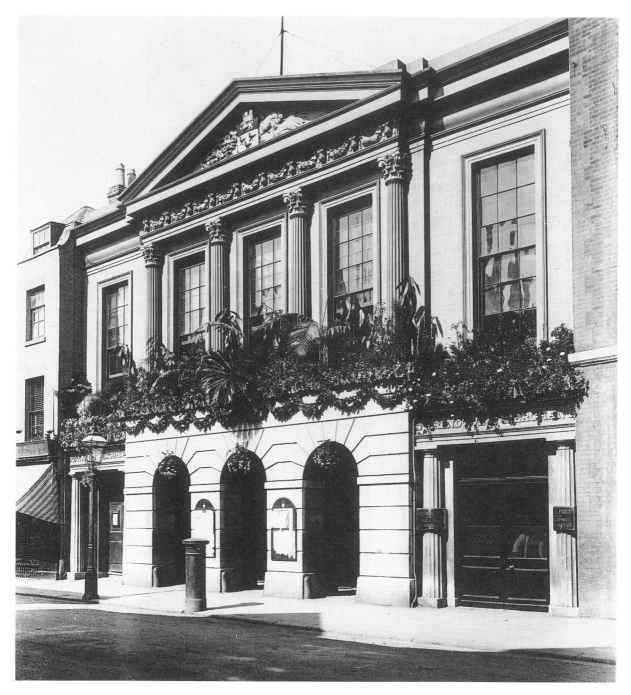

66 *Corn and Hop Exchange, High Street. Canterbury Archaeological Society fortunately commissioned a photographic record of the city's buildings before the 1942 air raid. This neo-classical facade to the Longmarket survived bombing only to be demolished; the Holden Plan's processional way was to have run here. See **81** for its contemporary replacement.*

67 *Dane John Gardens. George Vertue's print shows this civic amenity with Simmons' memorial on the mound. He gave the gardens to the city in disgust at receiving a bill for overdue poor rates of £8 after spending £1500 on their restoration.*

England', 'Gymnastics', 'Pneumatics', 'Entomology', 'Electricity' and 'The English Poets'. Beside St Radegund's Baths, chalybeate springs were frequented. Walks and arbours surrounded the paved well area now below Pound Lane car-park. The waters became clouded in air, so never acquired the cachet of Tunbridge Wells spa, although 'it is sovereign for . . . the stomach, rheumatic gouty pains, scurvy, melancholy distempers, vapours, stoppages, scab and itch . . . and agrees with old, weak and decayed constitutions'.

The poor

Before 1834, 14 parishes paid common poor rates and gave half-wage outdoor relief to over 2000 people in winter, a sixth of the population barely at subsistence level. The workhouse, at Poor Priests' Hospital since Elizabethan times, alongside the Bluecoat School, housed about 230 inmates, fed at 3s 8d a week each by private contractors who put them to public works. A

night's straw, bread and water were given to 2000 vagrants annually.

The high water-table, large numbers of intramural graveyards, lack of piped water and 60 back-street abattoirs were blamed by Dr Rigden, of the Canterbury Dispensary, for the poor health of overcrowded riverside parishioners, dying ten years younger than those at the top end of the town. Agues, fevers, pulmonary and rheumatic complaints plagued the 1000 patients examined in 1836 at the Dispensary, an offshoot of the hospital founded by subscription in 1790. The present hospital moved in 1937 from its site opposite the Longport coach park.

Canterbury lost most eighteenth-century public buildings in the 1940s. The 1808 Courthouse, its door crowned with crossed fasces and cap of liberty was retained. Three times the number of its original complement of rick-burners, thieves and poachers now occupy the adjoining gaol, a model of modernity in 1827.

Topic: Fifteenth- to eighteenth-century timber-framed buildings

Fire, which swept the medieval city, still strikes today and makes the Canterbury Archaeological Trust's building recording work essential for accurate reconstruction. Excavation exposes the ground plans of two-bay halls, and an early first-floor hall survives at St Alphege Rectory, but most standing timber-framed buildings are of fifteenth-century or later date. Work for the Council's Conservation Department shows these adaptable prefabs altered for cramped sites, adapted to house particular trades and being modernized for the comfort, display or privacy of wealthier owners.

The frontage of Luke the Moneyer's stone house, 53 St Peter's Street, has remained at 10.92m (36ft) since a Christchurch rental of c. 1200. Its thick flint and chalk walls survive to wall-plate level on three sides. A pointed doorway leads to the two-bay aisled timber hall, added behind when William Cokyn founded a short-lived hospital there in 1203. Soot-coated cross-bracing, with notched lap joints and four aisle posts, remains, although John Thomas, point-maker, built a kitchen in 1529 in the rear end and clad the front half in magnificent 'parchemin' panelling, carved with grapes and the tools of his trade. A moulded plaster ceiling from the modernized frontage of 1582 exists in the present shop. Six clergy widows shared the premises from 1657 under John Cogan's will; when the hospital moved in 1870, the present brick frontage went up, effectively concealing its unique evolution.

The illustrations show a suburban inn incorporating an imported market hall (**68**) and a cramped city centre inn expanding backwards (**69**). Seventeenth-century conspicuous wealth is displayed in bargeboards and brackets nearby, or in Sun Street's brick nogging (**70**).

68 *The 'Maiden's Head', Wincheap. The early fifteenth-century hall, by the street market outside the Castle, was up-dated in the seventeenth century by inserting a first floor, when the building became an inn. Perhaps then also a square, freestanding, gabled building, jettied on all sides, of about 1500, was brought on site and butted against the hall's rear elevation and the roofs married. It probably became the brewhouse.*

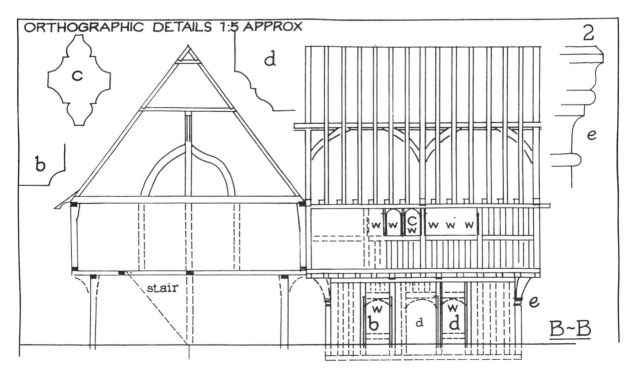

Eighteenth-century improvers brought flat fronts of brick, plaster or mathematical tiles with inserted sash windows to many earlier buildings.

Number 4–5 Best Lane, surveyed in 1992, reveals many of these processes in detail. It copies features of the great 'Cheker' Inn of 1392, although the first surviving lease is 1481. It was already old-fashioned, with a recessed open hall on the left and a possible shop and workshop in the two-storeyed section to the right of a through passage (**71**a). Its typical 'wealden' arch-brace, three original doorframes and a fine cinqfoil-headed window with vertical working shutter survive (**71**b). Behind the stairs to three upper chambers lay a contemporary three-bay kitchen extension with a smoke bay to roof level over a series of tiled hearths. Out of public view windows were simpler. This part retains its crown post, but from 1636 to 1839

69 *The Kentish Cricketers and 13 St Peter's Street. A fifteenth-century two-bay hall house on the street, was joined to its fourteenth-century neighbour at right angles. In 1723 a further three-bay extension was added northwards. Across St Peter's Lane, about 1600 a gabled house was built, with finely carved bargeboards, but only a smoke vent rather than the opulent later chimney.*

a succession of Walloon families, enjoying a fixed rent of 26s 8d per annum throughout, could afford alterations like chimney stacks in front.

Widow Maurois belonged to the Walloon élite; her successor Abraham Didier was a Canterbury merchant, but his son had migrated to Stepney by 1699, sub-letting to the LeKeux family, in residence until 1783. Samuel Lepine, next lessee, was a Freeman silk weaver who refaced the frontage in plaster with sash windows and added a third floor and new roof behind a parapet. With silk weaving declining,

70 *8 Sun Street. A late medieval three-storey building jettied on two sides, it has recently had its upper floor restored to its seventeenth-century appearance. The pairs of windows with pierced spandrels, carved heads and internal shutter-runners were uncovered, set in later herring-bone brick infilling.*

his son became a London builder and split the property into two dwellings in 1819.

A box-framed town house, bearing 1647 on its finial, is now handsomely restored at 28 Palace Street (**72**). The Trust's recording work identified the cause of a century of twist and list producing the much-photographed crooked door. A door, cut through a ground floor inglenook, fatally weakened the original brick chimney stack, rising from brick cellars, integral to the building's stability. Recorders were at

71 *4–5 Best Lane. The carved cinqfoil traceried window survived behind the plaster, below the oversailing roof at the side of the jetty. It had an intact sliding shutter pulled up from below and secured by a peg. There was evidence for other similar windows.*

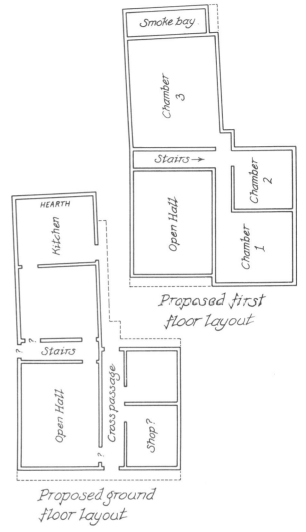

Proposed first floor layout

Proposed ground floor layout

work when the entire stack collapsed into the cellars, closing the street and necessitating massive shoring. Probably built for the weaver Alderman Sabine, its three storeys are jettied on two sides. Bay windows, bargeboards, mock stone plasterwork and elaborate brackets proclaimed its owner's wealth, yet it always incorporated a shop and additional windows would provide extra light for his weavers, working on material stored in the cellars.

Decorative brickwork had been used by the wealthy since the sixteenth century (**73**), but in real or mock tile-hung form it only became a common Canterbury sight during the refacing of the eighteenth century.

72 *28 Palace Street.*

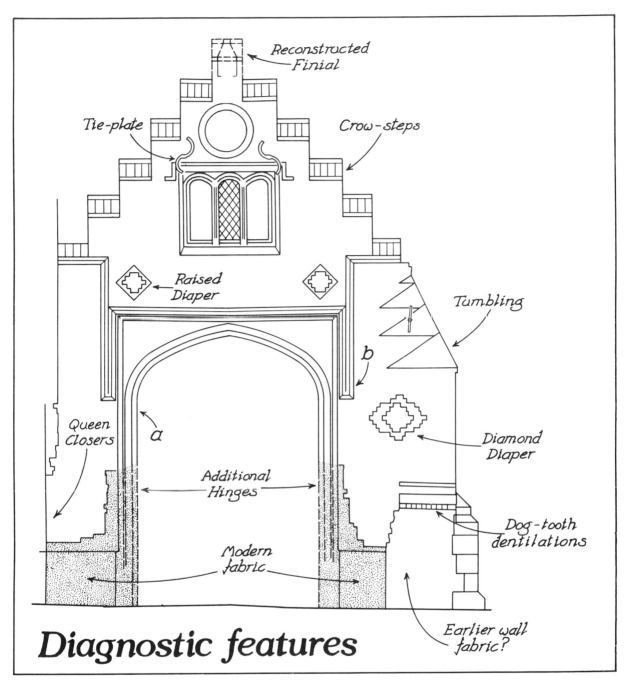

Reconstructed
Finial

Tie-plate

Crow-steps

Raised
Diaper

Tumbling

b

Queen
Closers

a

Diamond
Diaper

Additional
Hinges

Dog-tooth
dentilations

Modern
fabric

Earlier wall
fabric?

Diagnostic features

73 *Roper Gate c. 1550. All that remains of the Roper home incorporates, in the right buttress, bricks like those in the family chapel opposite. Diamond diapers, vitrified headers and 'tumbling' decorate this 'English bond' construction. Specially moulded bricks were hand-finished* in situ *for the crow-stepped gable and rounded mouldings.*

7

Survival and recovery

Canterbury owes its preservation to being a backwater once its railway failed. The recovery of its past began at St Augustine's and the Cathedral in the last century, and has accelerated since the Second World War through archaeology. Its revival owes much to education and tourism, but most to its old role as the economic and social hub of East Kent.

The Canterbury–Whitstable Railway

When railways were first mooted, local business leaders, like earlier canal promoters, still hoped to link Canterbury to the sea. They tackled the short but hilly route to Whitstable alone, rather than exploring joint promotion of a land link to London, and suffered the penalties of pioneers.

Simultaneous canal and railway Acts became law in June 1825. Both estimates were wildly optimistic, but the canal foundered while the railway, costing £83,000, opened within five years. The 28 local promoters needed to move heavy coal and agricultural produce quickly and cheaply, so persevered through 20 difficult years, with no dividend and an eventual return of one per cent on capital. Both Stephensons were actively involved in the project, but their *Invicta* locomotive needed several modifications and only ran on the flat central section. Stationary winding engines hauled wagons by cable up the inclines, consequently the tunnel under the modern University could not accommodate later more powerful locomotives

without damaging adaptations and asphyxiating fumes (**74**).

The railway scored several 'firsts', opening in May 1830, five months before its Liverpool–Manchester rival, to take freight and passengers at 9d for the forty-minute trip (**colour plate 11**). It boasted the first season tickets, combined boat/rail tickets and Sunday excursions, later stopped by local clergymen. The 1836 *Railway Companion* describes one of the ten weekday trips. Uncovered, single-class passenger carriages, with goods wagons behind as needed, left North Lane, Canterbury, at nine miles per hour to the top of Clowes Wood, with one change of cable. The hair-raising descent to Bogshole at 30 miles per hour was achieved by gravity without a cable. *Invicta* then steamed to Whitstable at 12 miles per hour, through 'country agreeably diversified' with views of the sea 'rolling in all the majesty of its rude and undulating nature'.

Transshipment caused delays and increased costs, for Whitstable's exposed roadstead was only expensively modernized with harbour works in 1832 and used sailing hoys until 1836, while Herne Bay operated steamboats to London. Repairs to *Invicta* and an extra winding engine drained profits. Contrary to expectations, more coal came in than goods went out, but customers benefited from competition with road haulage, £12,000 being saved in the first five years from moving 43,000 chaldrons of coal, 38,000 tons of goods and 69,305 people.

The line was leased out in 1838 but its lessees went bankrupt within three years and nobody would buy *Invicta*. The South-East Railway took on the line in 1844, running it until 1953.

Invicta is displayed in the Heritage Museum; the handsome West Station of 1844 is still open and stretches of the line can be walked, although the tunnel was filled in when University buildings above developed cracks. Originally closed at night lest it encouraged immorality and vice, the tunnel became an air-raid shelter in the 1940s, without any recorded moral danger.

'New wine in old bottles' – education revived

Henry VIII's underused Palace on the St Augustine's site came to the Hales family by 1658, who preserved the estate intact until hospital, courthouse and gaol buildings began in 1791 a break-up completed by 1808. A brewery ran a tavern and pleasure ground in the Outer Court (see **12**). Rumbling protests culminated in a letter to *The English Churchman* in 1843 which caught the eye of the wealthy young MP for Maidstone, John Beresford Hope. After a first horrified visit to Canterbury the following week, he eventually managed to lease the Outer Court for 2000 guineas. Thus began a tediously long battle to rescue the whole area for religious use, linking a new educational foundation to the first abbey of 598.

Beresford Hope and Edward Coleridge established a Missionary College in 1848, commissioning William Butterfield to restore and enlarge the medieval buildings. Recovering and excavating cloister and churches took another century of appeals to antiquarian benefactors, but new priorities for church education ended the Missionary College in 1946. Christchurch College now occupies the northern site, the King's School owns the Court and English Heritage has guardianship of the archaeological area. Archaeology had begun in 1845, but the main excavations ran from 1900 to 1930, as land acquisition and funds permitted. This long campaign of vision, persistence and skill found

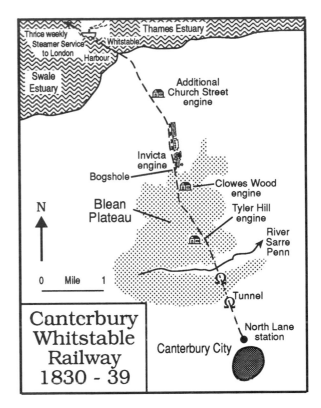

74 *Route of the Canterbury–Whitstable Railway. Originally,* Invicta *ran from Bogshole to Whitstable but a third winding engine became necessary. After a harbour replaced the roadstead, in 1832, sailing hoys and steamers both used Whitstable.*

undaunted protagonists, seeing themselves as St Augustine's heirs; this complicated site must now be made to speak to modern tourists.

Until 1880 schooling for most local children ended around ten. Canterbury resembled most old towns; its King's School had changed since Marlowe's day and was now the preserve of middle-class feepayers aiming for the professions and the universities. Ancient endowments supported the city Bluecoat School alongside the workhouse in the old Poor Priests' Hospital, and others at Jesus and Eastbridge hospitals aimed at apprenticing poor boys. In 1881 all these endowments were incorporated into the new Middle Schools for boys and girls on strictly segregated parts of the Whitefriars site. Scholarship children from elementary schools and feepayers were to gain 'a good, sound, English education, suitable for those who would have to enter a commercial line of life'. This traditional method of achieving a modern education was Canterbury's way of following a nationwide trend. Despite the lead given by the Dean and the King's School headmaster, the schools were never denominational. The city had attracted the Clergy Orphans' School, St Edmunds, joined in 1885 by the Methodist Kent College. The Simon Langton Grammar Schools, their Whitefriars home largely destroyed in 1942, flourish on new sites, their name recalling the medieval benefactions from which they began.

Monuments to 'self-help'

Two remarkable self-made Victorians left buildings to modern Canterbury. Sidney Cooper's cottage stands by the Ionic portico of the Cooper Centre in St Peter's Street (**75**). His deserted mother raised five children there, by dressmaking, to see one son become Mayor of Canterbury, the other a rich and famous Royal Academician. Cooper bought the cottage and founded his art school in her memory in 1867 'to encourage young talent and provide the facilities I had been denied in my youth', teaching there weekly for years. Archbishop Manners-Sutton had given £5 to the boy sketching in the precincts, which 'gave me faith in mankind to persevere in taking up an artistic career'. Cooper exhibited annually at the Royal Academy from 1833 to 1902. Queen Victoria commissioned a cow portrait in 1848; Edward VII bought a painting for his grandchildren's Sandringham nursery in 1901. He built a theatre, rescued mills and donated open space since 'it gave me pleasure to do what I could for the old place'. The modern art college, his animal paintings at the Museum, and his magnificent lithographs of Cathedral and City are his legacy (see **12** and **colour plate 10**).

Sidney's brother George and Dr Rigden of the Dispensary in turn helped a local labourer's son, James Beaney, to study medicine in Edin-

burgh. A chequered career as army and ship's surgeon and failed chemist landed him in gold-rush Melbourne in 1857. By 1891 he was earning three times the fees of his rivals, who used patients' deaths under public surgery and his books on venereal disease to attack the flashy lifestyle of 'Diamond Jimmy' in long-running scandalous controversies. Neglecting his pauper sister, he left £10,000 to the city for the flamboyant Beaney Institute 'for the education of the Labouring Man', now shared by the County Library and the Royal Museum. The Cathedral received £1000 to erect his elaborate memorial in the nave.

Canterbury and the blitz

In 1939, old patterns apparently survived, untouched by industrialization. Family shops, in narrow lanes and streets with some modern brick among timber jetties, catered for an already old-fashioned social mix. Sometimes things happened: the parliamentary borough was disfranchised for corruption in 1853 and 1880; a fire in 1865 destroyed two-thirds of the Cheker Inn; serious floods periodically inundated cottages near Westgate. To the weekly cattle-market and annual cricket week were added four cinemas. From 1928 the Cathedral Festival plays revived a moribund tradition of religious drama with commissions like Eliot's *Murder in the Cathedral* and Dorothy Sayers' *Zeal of Thy House*.

Change was already afoot with a proposed ring-road. Opening the Broad Street car-park in 1931, the Labour leader George Lansbury congratulated the Council on its housing programme of 1000 houses in ten years, prophesying to listening children 'in your lifetime, every unfit house will go'. The cast of mind which sentenced to demolition premises outliving their useful span wrought more destruction in the 1950s and 1960s than the Luftwaffe in 1942.

75 *Cooper's cottage and gallery. Sidney Cooper, R.A.'s first home and his art school are now the Chaucer Centre and community halls. The pinched classical portico has been copied at the entrance to the new Roman Museum.*

Canterbury had received London refugees before the fall of France prompted a second exodus. If invasion came, Home Guard and Army were to defend the city to the end from its medieval walls. German bombers in trouble dropped occasional loads, but raids on historic cities like Exeter, in April 1942, alerted Council and citizens that, despite well-rehearsed preparations, their close-packed medieval town was very vulnerable.

From 12.45 to 2.10a.m. on 1 June 1942, a hundred high-explosive and thousands of incendiary bombs rained down, heralded by 16 blood-red flares. Fortunately for the Cathedral they drifted on the night wind to cluster on St George's parish at the eastern end of the High Street. Corn Exchange and Longmarket, two churches, most of the Simon Langton Grammar Schools and the Cathedral Library were lost and 48 people died. At the Cathedral, glass and library treasures had been removed and the crypt shelter cushioned with earth. Firefighters tossed incendiaries from the roof but bombs ringed the building, demolishing most of Burgate and damaging precincts and King's School buildings.

Three more raids followed but, lying between flight paths, Canterbury largely escaped doodlebugs and V2 rockets. In 135 separate raids, 10,445 bombs destroyed 731 homes, killed 115 people and demolished 296 other buildings. Today, looking east from Longmarket, only the tower of St George's church is pre-war (**76**).

76 *St George's Street, June 1942. Taken from the surviving roof of Marks and Spencer's, this view of bomb damage shows how much of the heat-scorched fabric of the church where Marlowe was baptized survived for ruthless demolition. The tower remains in a 1992 redevelopment, where excavation reached the level of a probable Roman temple precinct. Frere's post-war excavation of a Roman bath-house occurred in the left-hand cellars, now Woolworths.*

Planning battles

Dean Hewlett Johnson's uncompromising Communist views and actions still obscure his work in rescuing monastic remains, restoring the Cathedral fabric and reviving the King's School, like his Victorian predecessors Alford and Farrar. Staying throughout the raids and opening the Deanery's bomb-scarred doors to the homeless, he won local admiration. In July 1942, with the Mayor and Archbishops Temple and Lang, he wrote to *The Times* urging that private interest be subordinated in post-war planning, to set the Cathedral 'like a jewel' in the city. In 1945 the resulting Holden Plan produced uproar (**77**). The city would buy 75 central acres, obliterating ancient boundaries, to secure open vistas of the Cathedral from a new processional way along the western edge of the bombed area. Widespread demolition would follow. A new relief road, bisecting the city parallel to the High Street, would supplement an inner ring-road and outer by-pass. The Citizens' Defence Association, in revolt, won the municipal elections, so only 35 acres (14 ha) were purchased, undistinguished 'contemporary' shops were erected on old plots, but surface car-parks remained for years as money ran out. Slum clearance removed cottages and lanes, now regretted, but established well-planned council estates and schools. St George's Terrace, the Guildhall and the *Fleur de Lys* hotel were deemed beyond restoration; moat and cattlemarket were sacrificed to the inner ring-road.

77 *The Holden Plan. This 1967 map of the modified Holden Plan accompanied Lewis Braithwaite's critical article 'Canterbury: historic town or write-off?'. Dr Holden, working on the City of London plan, devised a 1940s traffic solution akin to bombed Exeter's. His processional way has gone but the bisecting relief road stands, then still unaccompanied by a by-pass. Pedestrianization was to save the inner city.*

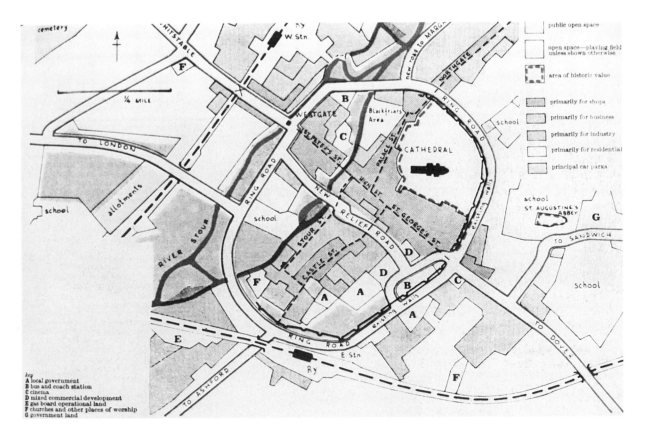

Country Life in 1945 had feared 'the result of petty individualism may be not to attract but to repel visitors from a city that may become famous not for its beauty but as a traffic bottleneck'! The Buchanan Report addressed these problems which remained unresolved throughout the 1970s. Completing the inner ring-road would maroon the Westgate on a traffic island and isolate St Dunstan's Street; only in 1982 did the by-pass divert Dover traffic from the city walls. Traffic between Thanet and Ashford still clogs the approaches and ring-roads.

The rediscovery of Canterbury

Canterbury's Roman origins were common knowledge to the Elizabethans, Lambarde and Camden, but remains were not described until native-born William Somner first identified Roman gates, relating them to Kent's road plan in his *Antiquities of Canterbury* (1640). These gates were drawn or recorded by Stukeley and Gostling before their eighteenth-century demolition, but revived antiquarian interest brought the British Archaeological Association to Canterbury for its first meeting in 1844. By their next visit, in 1929, much more was known about the cemeteries and the eastern walls, but speculation on topography, following Pilbrow's discoveries while laying main drainage, favoured the mistaken idea that the Roman city never spread westwards across the eastern branch of the Stour. The 1932 Victoria County History perpetuated this myth.

When the eastern half of the city was flattened in 1942, the Canterbury Excavation Committee was soon formed (**78**). The first urban 'rescue' excavations in Britain began in 1944 under Audrey Williams. Short of money, using volunteers and pressed by shopkeepers desperate to rebuild, she and her successor Sheppard Frere used spring and summer holidays to excavate, mainly in cellars, every year until 1957. These explorations revolutionized knowledge, for a chronology from Iron Age Belgae to fifth-century Jutes was established by the first detailed stratigraphic sequences. Enough large sections of buildings were found to draw plans of houses, baths and theatre and thereby to form a provisional street grid (**79**). It was at last demonstrated that the entire medieval wall circuit sat on Roman foundations. The fine mosaic pavement, found below Butchery Lane in 1946, was preserved and is displayed in the enlarged Roman Museum below Longmarket, where visitors can study the collected artefacts of Durovernum. John Boyle's and John Wacher's discovery of early Anglo-Saxon pottery and sunken huts below the Langton schools at Whitefriars ended this period in 1960.

Dr Frank Jenkins could only keep watch and undertake small rescue operations during the 1960s and 1970s; fortunately in 1975 the Canterbury Archaeological Trust was born, just as a spate of new development began, providing opportunities for large-scale area excavations. At last this ancient city, receiving two million visitors annually, had a full-time professional unit to excavate and publish, its principal object being 'the advancement of public education in the subject of archaeology'.

The historic core within the walls and its ancient suburbs together was one of the first areas designated under the Archaeological Areas Act, where excavation must occur before

78 *Aerial view of Canterbury in 1942. This shows the Roman wall line, the Saxon inner burh round the Cathedral and close-packed medieval city beside the concentrated area of bomb damage. Post-war excavation began in the centre; Jutish traces were later found on the Whitefriars site (bottom left) where part of the Langton schools survived. The Trust started area excavation in 1977–8 at the extreme left.*

79 *Sheppard Frere's plan of St George's bath-house. Measured buildings, dated in sequence, revolutionized local archaeology. Cramped work in four bombed cellars produced this drawing of a bath-house of no earlier than 200–25, above second-century and Iron Age levels. The building had been altered before fire destroyed it around 360.*

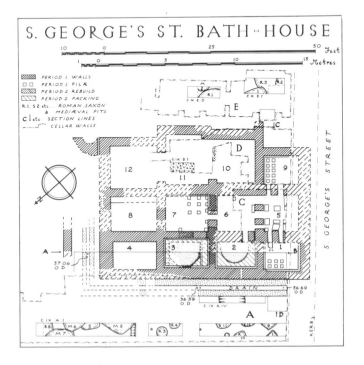

S. GEORGE'S ST. BATH-HOUSE

redevelopment. The Trust's first two Directors have developed such close working relations with the Conservation and Planning Departments of the new District Council that archaeology is built into both these processes, above and below ground. Given that one seventh of the city centre was redeveloped in the following 15 years, it was vital that the Trust was on the spot as swathes of the Roman, Saxon and medieval city, the precincts and the Lanfranc sites in Northgate were laid bare and surviving timber-framed buildings were refurbished.

Despite recurrent, severe financial crises, the Trust has acquired its freehold headquarters and a shop, a Friends organization, an increasingly computerized archive and an enviable reputation for publication, both academic and popular. Cooperation with English Heritage has been as vital here as that with the Council on the ground. Outside the city, the Trust conducted the Eurotunnel Terminal excavations and consequent watching briefs for the Department of Transport which, in 1993, brought to light the amazing Dover Bronze Age boat.

Tourism and the future

The new District Council in 1974 incorporated countryside and coastal towns with the city of Canterbury, and has to balance its national and international importance as a tourist centre containing three 'World Heritage' sites with the needs of its area, particularly Whitstable and Herne Bay. The Kent Structure Plan also limits the size and nature of the city's development. Attitudes have changed through the experience of managing the flood of day visitors and their vehicles, without destroying what they come to see. The city centre is largely pedestrianized and, after two hotly-contested forerunners in the 1970s, no more multi-storey car-parks breach the line of city walls. Buildings and streetscapes have been sensitively restored, not least the Heritage Museum in the Poor Priests' Hospital. St Alphege and St Margaret's churches serve new needs as an Urban Studies Centre and 'The Canterbury Tales' experience.

These and the three other museums tempt tourists to explore the city beyond the Cathedral and enjoy the riverside and city wall walks; the May and October Chaucer and Canterbury Festivals and the Marlowe Theatre programme spread them throughout the year. This would please the 'Red Dean' who campaigned in the 1930s for these ends. Most visitors are aged between 35 and 54, in the upper socio-economic groups and stay only one to three nights. They are usually *en route* elsewhere, on a first and probably only visit; in 1985 they spent £45 million. These figures pinpoint future challenges.

Tourism creates a wider range of shops and services than a town of this size could expect, so massive shopping developments have roused new debate as contemporary styles and materials are replaced by derivative ones (**80** and **81**). Residents regret the passing of their small-town community and fight proposals which would exclude housing from the old centre. Apart from tourism and retail distribution, education is the largest employer. Three independent schools, ten language schools, the University of Kent at Canterbury and Christchurch College all press on local accommodation, while Canterbury College and the Kent Institute of Art and Design draw their students from a 30-mile (51 km) radius. Canterbury with this tripod of functions is reasonably well placed to face the uncertainties of its third millennium; past history suggests that its citizens will find answers to its problems.

Topic: The University of Kent at Canterbury

Since Theodore's school in the late 600s, the dream of Canterbury as a centre of learning has lingered, through Archbishop Baldwin's abortive Hackington College in the twelfth century and Cranmer's hopes of a scholarly foundation in 1540. The nineteenth century brought the city an Anglican missionary College, an art school, two boarding schools, the Simon Langton Grammar Schools and the revival of the King's School, each founder part-

motivated by Canterbury's ancient tradition. When university expansion was canvassed in the 1950s, the city, at 31,000, was thought to be too small and too poorly connected by road and rail to London; even when sites were first examined, two nearby stately homes or a Thanet site seemed preferable. It seemed that Christchurch, an Anglican training college, already rising on St Augustine's land, would be the only new foundation.

Yet Canterbury's amenities for staff and accommodation for students were prominent components of the County's submission, accepted by the government in May 1961. John Boyle, Town Clerk and a keen archaeologist, was a key figure in speeding the project, owing to the complexity of the legal status of land on the proposed site. The University's cumbersome title reflects the partnership of the County and a city, then still a County Borough. Dr Geoffrey Templeman became first Vice-Chancellor in August 1962 and the first full student intake arrived in October 1965, a rapid progress putting immense strain on all concerned.

The location seemed ideal, with some 200–

80 *Sainsbury's in 1993. A competition-winning entry in 1982, this design by Ahrends, Burton and Koralek won Industrial Steel Design and Civic Trust Awards in 1985 and 1986. It stands on Domesday Book's King's Meadow, where later travelling circuses erected 'Big Tops'.*

300 acres (80–120 ha) of poor agricultural land, sparsely occupied, near to but not in the city, its funding guaranteed by two authorities. Hasted could have warned them: 'stiff clay and cold loam, both wet and miry'. No ground as high can be found until 500 miles east of St Petersburg, whence the wind blows. In fact the site involved five separate local authorities and 20 owners, some old charitable trusts like St John's Hospital. Sports facilities were to be sited where Town and Gown met and be the centre of gravity where cordial relations would grow. These 37 acres (15 ha) nearest to the city proved too expensive, a severe blow which marooned the University on its hill, where compensatory land was bought from Eastbridge Hospital. Away from the city, science buildings, sports hall and student housing have since mushroomed (**82**).

81 *Longmarket: Land Securities plc 1992. Robert Semple of Building Design Partnership, advised by Anthony Swaine, balanced commercial, aesthetic and amenity demands to produce this well-crafted if over-large design once public consultation identified strong demand for retaining the open square of the post-war era. The other three sides match the medieval, Georgian and modern buildings they face.*

Templeman's vision of a collegiate university of 5000 in eight colleges was also practical. The provision of lecture and seminar rooms, accommodation and catering as each modular college was completed meant that only the library, laboratories, registry and boilerhouse had to be provided at once. This thinking still affects today's developments, when students prefer housing to communal living and funding cuts have only allowed four colleges to be built. However, a collegiate university demanded a single architect to design a total concept for the whole site, capable of modification and infilling

as academic needs and government priorities changed. Sir William Holford, then President of the RIBA, was chosen, a South African who had worked on Canberra and Brasilia. He set his stamp on the campus from November 1961 to mid-1965 (**83**). In Professor Bann's words, 'The Holford scheme was like a series of grandiloquent words displayed in bold capitals across a page with considerable space between them. Henderson [his successor] has attempted to make sentences out of the isolated words'. Thirty years later, tree planting has humanized the buildings but, whether viewed from campus or city, the image of the University on the hill is Holford's.

His brief stay arose from the inevitable tensions of an impossibly tight timescale and budget. New professors received building plans with their appointment letters with little time for modifications. With few 'users' in place, university administrators on top of their normal

urgent concerns felt impelled to oversee design processes. Unlike contemporary Essex, they had only a derelict farmhouse and two city buildings as temporary headquarters. Holford was often called away and had expected to handle design and execution down to contractor level. Yet when he left, the first library block and Eliot College were built and its mirror, Rutherford College, was begun. With Anthony Wade, he planned colleges round dining halls commanding magnificent Cathedral views (**colour plate 12**). Sets of rooms on short closeable, corridors echoed Oxbridge staircases, as did internal quadrangles. Although built of vertical concrete panels, the form of each college is a Greek cross. He planned a central campanile for vertical emphasis but now the pagoda-like Senate House crouches before the Templeman Library. Sponsored research programmes, electronics and computing, drama and music, joint degree courses,

82 *Aerial view of U.K.C. campus 1990. Holford's Library and two colleges occupy the centre, flanked by Keynes and Darwin Colleges. The road from left to right, not Holford's road, is the main artery with science buildings beyond. Student housing rather than four new colleges now spreads even further northwards (top left). The central footpath leads downhill to a housing estate occupying the sports area planned to link town and gown.*

many related to European studies, demonstrate the University's connection with the wider world. Perhaps because of the site's isolation, academics strive to contribute to every aspect of city life. Canterbury benefits not only from jobs and cultural facilities but also from the injection of young life and attitudes into the hardening arteries of an old city. A Japanese institution in Korean style has recently arisen opposite the Cathedral on the University slope. In Canterbury fashion, its name is Chaucer College.

115

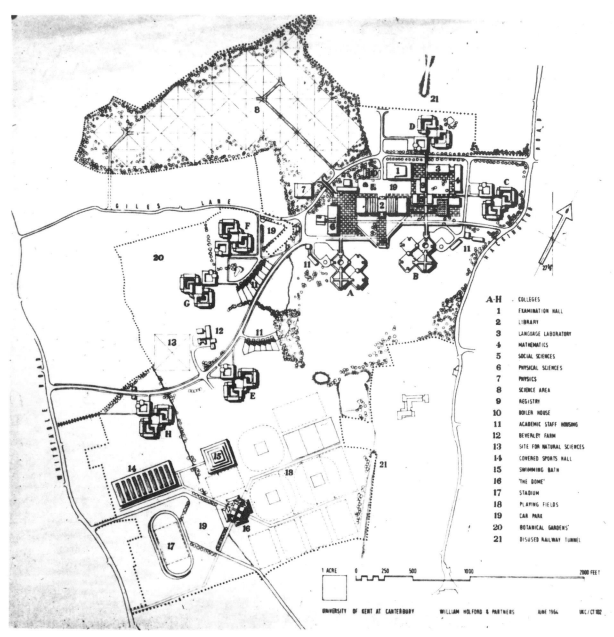

A-H — COLLEGES
1 EXAMINATION HALL
2 LIBRARY
3 LANGUAGE LABORATORY
4 MATHEMATICS
5 SOCIAL SCIENCES
6 PHYSICAL SCIENCES
7 PHYSICS
8 SCIENCE AREA
9 REGISTRY
10 BOILER HOUSE
11 ACADEMIC STAFF HOUSING
12 BEVERLEY FARM
13 SITE FOR NATURAL SCIENCES
14 COVERED SPORTS HALL
15 SWIMMING BATH
16 'THE DOME'
17 STADIUM
18 PLAYING FIELDS
19 CAR PARK
20 BOTANICAL GARDENS
21 DISUSED RAILWAY TUNNEL

1 ACRE   0   250   500   1000   2000 FEET

UNIVERSITY OF KENT AT CANTERBURY   WILLIAM HOLFORD & PARTNERS   JUNE 1964   UKC/CT 102

83 *Holford's plan for U.K.C. 1964. Comparison with **82** shows how the cost of land to the south, funding cuts and changed students' attitudes to communal living have altered the original concept of a collegiate university linked to Canterbury.*

What to visit in Canterbury

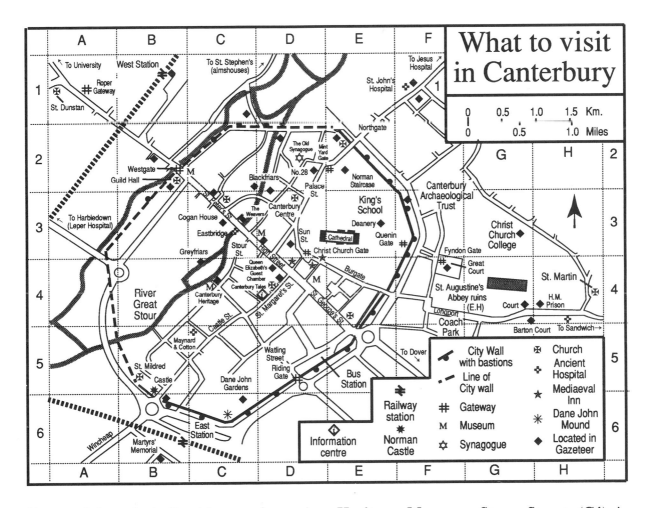

What to visit in Canterbury

| 0 | 0.5 | 1.0 | 1.5 Km. |
| 0 | | 0.5 | 1.0 Miles |

Map labels:
To University · West Station · To St. Stephen's (almshouses) · To Jesus Hospital · St. John's Hospital · Roper Gateway · St. Dunstan · Northgate · The Old Synagogue · Mint Yard Gate · No.28 · Norman Staircase · Canterbury Archaeological Trust · Westgate · Guild Hall · Blackfriars · Palace St. · King's School · Christ Church College · To Harbledown (Leper Hospital) · Cogan House · The Weavers · Canterbury Centre · Deanery · Christ Church Gate · St. Martin · Eastbridge · Sun St. · Cathedral · Quenin Gate · Fyndon Gate · Great Court · Greyfriars · Stour St. · Queen Elizabeth's Guest Chamber · St. Augustine's Abbey ruins (E.H) · Court · H.M. Prison · River Great Stour · Canterbury Heritage · Canterbury Tales · St. Margaret's St. · Longport · Coach Park · Barton Court · To Sandwich · Maynard & Cotton · Castle St. · St. George's St. · Burgate · St. Mildred · Castle · Dane John Gardens · Watling Street · Riding Gate · Bus Station · To Dover · East Station · Martyrs' Memorial · Wincheap · High Street

Legend:
City Wall with bastions · Line of City wall · Railway station · Gateway · Museum · Synagogue · Information centre · Norman Castle · Church · Ancient Hospital · Mediaeval Inn · Dane John Mound · Located in Gazeteer

(Arranged chronologically with map references)
Tourist Information Centre, St Margaret's Street (**D4**) is located in an interesting seventeenth-century house, repaired after an archaeological survey, following fire. Guided tours start here and booklets are on sale.

Heritage Museum, Stour Street (**C4**) is housed in the thirteenth-century Poor Priests' Hospital (see pp. 74–6 for its chequered history). Apart from the magnificent building, the overview of Canterbury's history is imaginatively displayed with objects as diverse as the seventh-century gold pendant (**back cover**) and *Invicta* locomotive (pp. 104–5). It is open daily, except on Good Friday and Christmas Day, from 10.30a.m. to 4p.m. but only on Sundays from June to October, 1.30 to 4p.m.

Roman

Roman Museum, Butchery Lane (**D4**) (Opening hours as at the Heritage Museum.) An enlarged area below modern shops contains the mosaic floor found in 1946 (p. 110), Roman artefacts from around the city and an education room.

Queningate, Broad Street Car Park (**F3**) This blocked gate (p. 42) can be traced to the right of the present steps to the Memorial Gardens just before the square fourteenth-century bastion.

St Mary Northgate Wall, behind 72 Northgate (**E2**) (see p. 40) The blocked Norman window sits on the merlon of Roman crenellations which can then be traced along the wall. Below them most material is Roman, *c.* 270.

Dane John Mound (**C6**) (see pp. 57–8) Although altered from Norman times onward, it is a survivor from a pre-270 Roman cemetery, as is the Canterbury Motor Company's mound, opposite across the ring road.

Roman Ridingate (**D5**) Foundations outlined in red in the roadway (**Colour plates 2** and **3**).

Saxon

St Martin's Church, St Martin's Hill (**H4**) is usually open in daylight hours (see pp. 50–2).

St Augustine's Abbey, Longport (**F/G4**) English Heritage, open summer daily 10a.m. to 1p.m. and 2 to 6p.m.; winter, closes at 4p.m., and shuts on Mondays and public holidays (see pp. 50–3).

St Mildred's Church, behind the Castle (**B5**) can also be viewed from the ring road. It is usually shut but the south wall with long- and short-work angles is typically late Saxon (see p. 49).

Norman

The Castle, Castle Street (**B5**) (no internal admittance) (see pp. 58–9).

St Augustine's Abbey see above.

'Norman Staircase', Green Court, King's School (**E2**) This external stair, originally surmounted by the last cistern of Prior Wibert's water system (see **colour plate 6**), leads to the surviving half of his '*Aula Nova*', the guest hall beside his **Gate** from the Mint Yard, *c.* 1160. His **Treasury**, **Infirmary Chapel** and **Cloister** and **Watertower** are seen on touring the north side of the precincts. The **Western Crypt** and the Norman parts of the Cathedral surviving the fire of 1174 are covered by Cathedral guides. Enquire at the Welcome Centre.

'Theodore' Education department in the north-west corner of the Cloisters has an audio-visual programme and material for young visitors, e.g. a Monks' Trail.

St John's Hospital, Northgate (**F1**) This Lanfranc foundation can usually be visited in daylight hours. Parts of the dormitory and the necessarium can be seen. The surviving part of the chapel is heavily altered and the almshouses are later (see p. 68).

St Gregory's Priory site opposite awaits development (see p. 69).

St Nicholas' Hospital, Harbledown (**off A3**) Lanfranc's leper hospital's church retains late Norman work but almshouse, gatehouse and hall are later.

Eastbridge Hospital, High Street (**C3**) (see p. 74) Undercroft, hall and chapel can be visited from Monday to Saturday from 10a.m. to 5p.m.

Medieval
Friaries

The remaining **Greyfriars building** (**C4**) can be viewed from the riverside walk.

Dominican Guest Hall, St Peter's Lane (**C2**) This fourteenth-century building, now a community centre, can be viewed from the adjoining public orchard with the surviving thirteenth-century *frater*, now the King's School Arts Centre, on the opposite bank (see p. 72). The Precinct Gate is depicted above the Spastics Shop on the corner of the Friars in St Peter's Street (**C3**).

Churches

St Alphege, Palace Street (**D2**) is open from 10.30a.m. to 5p.m. Wednesday to Saturday. It is the Canterbury Centre for Urban Studies, containing displays, revolving multi-media exhibitions on Canterbury's buildings, children's and adults' walking trails and other material for sale. Light refreshments and toilets available.

St Margaret's, St Margaret's Street (**D4**) now houses 'The Canterbury Tales', a modern theme experience of pilgrimage in Chaucer's day. It is open daily throughout the year and has a large shop and education packs.

St Peter's, St Peter's Street (**C3**) shows an early tower base of mixed material. If open, it is interesting for the early west end of the nave and the post-Black Death north aisle. It is flanked by the 'Kentish Cricketers' and Hubble's sports shop (see p. 99).

Vanished churches are marked by plaques (St Mary Bredman and St Andrew, High Street), red pavement outline (All Saints', opposite the Post Office) or by towers (St George and St Mary Magdalene, Burgate).

Detached **churchyards** survive at St Mary de Castro, Castle Street (**C5**) and St Mary Northgate, the Royal Dragoons pub garden, Military Road (**F2**)

Defences

Westgate (1380, see p. 78) (**B2**) now houses a museum relating to its history as the city gaol. Open Monday to Saturday 11a.m. to 12.30p.m. and 1.30 to 3.30p.m. **Holy Cross Church** beside it is now the City Guildhall and is not open.

Tower House, Westgate Gardens (**B2**), adjoining to the south and two bastion towers to the north in Pound Lane survive as houses.

Walls are best viewed from Broad Street car park (**F3**) and Dane John Gardens (**C6**) (see p.57). The ring road truncated the city ditch.

Pilgrim Inns

High Street to Burgate (**D4**) (see p. 81ff.). Standing on one corner of St Margaret's Street, one Inn is behind you and Ratner's corner of **The Cheker of the Hope** in front, with cellar grilles, stone base and surviving window high on the Mercery Lane face. Before the fire of 1865 it stretched to Debenham's, whose buttery restaurant is in the cellar of another Inn. After viewing **The Sun Inn** (Pizzaland and Cathedral Gate Hotel) observe from Burgate the size of **The White Bull** incorporating all the shops from the Buttermarket to Butchery Lane where remains of its yard open to the right.

Houses

Stowaways Restaurant, St Peter's Street (**C3**) (see p. 98) hides Canterbury's earliest house behind its brick facade.

All Saints' Court, off St Peter's Street (**C3**) is a late medieval row under a continuous jetty, as is George's Brasserie (**C4**) in Castle Street.

Sixteenth and seventeenth centuries

Most exposed timber-framed houses, e.g. **St Dunstan's Street** and **North Lane** (**B2**) or the **Swan, Northgate** (**F1**) are of this date. Many more hide behind frontages modernized in the eighteenth century. Number **28 Palace Street** (**D2**) (see p. 102) must be viewed, as well as the **weavers' houses** there and on King's Bridge (**C3**).

Brick buildings. The gateway to the **Roper house** in St Dunstan's Street (**A1**) has been restored recently near St Dunstan's Church where the brick **Roper Chapel** houses the memorial to Sir Thomas More, Margaret Roper's father (see pp. 86 and 103).

The Deanery (**E3**) is the earliest surviving large brick edifice for, in 1542, the New Foundation retained the late fifteenth-century Prior's Lodging.

16 Watling Street (D5)

The earliest brick town house surviving belonged to the Man family. Although modernized in the eighteenth century, it retains its projecting *garderobe* (lavatory) at the side.

The brick arch beside **Fyndon's Gate** (**F4**) at St Augustine's Abbey relates to Henry VIII's King's Lodging and brick nogging is exposed at **8 Sun Street** (**D3**). **Jesus Hospital**, **Sturry Road**, (**off F1**) and **Manwood Almshouses, St Stephen's Green** (**off B1**) are brick charitable assemblages described on p. 90.

John and Anne Smith Almshouses, St Martin's Hill (**H4**) are 1657 with a Flemish gable.

Pargetting as on **Queen Elizabeth's Restaurant, High Street** (**D4**) is rare in Canterbury.

The memorial with all the **Marian Martyrs** listed on it is in Martyr's Field Road (**B6**). (see p. 89)

Eighteenth century

Dane John Gardens (**C6**) is the only surviving civic amenity. Laid out by Alderman James Simmons, his memorial obelisk crowns the mound. Regency houses line the western limits.

Fish market portico, St Margaret's Street (**D4**) is unfortunately partly obscured by one of its two modern shops.

Mills

Some remnants of **Smeaton's** machinery (**D2**) (see p. 95) remain opposite The Miller's Arms and **Miller's Field** car-park (**D1**) is opposite sheltered housing at Hooker's Mill. Both were burned this century.

Maynard and Cotton's Hospital, off Castle Street (**C5**) is a medieval foundation rebuilt in 1708 on a modest scale.

Houses refaced in brick or mathematical tiles are best seen in **St Peter's Street** (**C3**)

Isolated Georgian houses are **St Peter's House** (**C3**), **Westgate House** (**B2**), and **Barton Court, Longport, 1750** (**H4**) now a school.

The **Courthouse and Prison** opposite, 1808, replaced the **Old Sessions House** near the Castle (**B6**).

Nineteenth century

West Station (**B1**), 1846. The South Eastern Railway's new terminus after the collapse of the Canterbury–Whitstable Railway Company whose original site is at the nearby coalyard, due for redevelopment.

Butterfield's 1848 Lodgings and Great Hall (**F4**) round St Augustine's Court (**G3**), now owned by the King's School, can be viewed through the entrance arch.

St Edmund's School, 1854–5, St Thomas' Hill (**off A1**) built by Hardwick for the Clergy Orphan Foundation in handsome Victorian Decorated style.

The Synagogue, King Street (**D2**), now the King's School Music Room, was built in Egyptian style as the second post-medieval centre for local Jews. It remained in use until 1939. The Canterbury Centre sells a Jewish Trail for other Jewish sites.

The portico of **Sidney Cooper's Art School, St Peter's Street** (**C3**) and the **Beaney Institute, 1897, High Street** (**D3**), now a Library, Art Gallery and Regimental Museum (see p. 106).

Twentieth century
Eliot and Rutherford Colleges, U.K.C. 1964–5 (**off A1**) (see p. 115).

Christchurch College, North Holmes Road, 1962–4 (**G3**) The chapel has a surprising four-gabled glazed roof.

A variety of early post-war shops co-exist in **St George's Street** (**E4**), flanked by 1989–93 redevelopments in derivative styles.

Whitefriars, Riceman's and the multi-storey car-park (**D5**) are unhappy reminders of the 1960s and 1970s.

Sainsbury's prizewinning design in Kingsmead provokes admiration or loathing but never indifference (**off E1**) (see p. 113).

Canterbury Archaeological Trust, 92a Broad Street (**F3**). Popular and scholarly publications, continually used in this book, and educational material for schools are available for sale during weekday working hours.

Further Reading

Canterbury impinges on so many fields of study that this list can only be an introduction. Several out-of-print books are worth seeking in libraries and second-hand shops. They include:

William Urry's *Canterbury under the Angevin Kings* (1967) and *Christopher Marlowe and Canterbury* (ed. Butcher 1988); Urry also edited William Somner's *Antiquities of Canterbury* (1976). Frank Barlow's *Thomas Becket* (1986) is authoritative. The first woman Mayor, Catherine Williamson, wrote *Though the Streets Burn* (1966) which describes the years 1939 to 1944, and the views of John Boyle, archaeologist and Town Clerk 1942–1972, come across in *The Illustrated Portrait of Canterbury* (1988). Robert Willis' *Architectural History of Canterbury Cathedral* (1845) contains Eadmer's account of the pre-Conquest Cathedral and Gervase's account of the fire and rebuilding from 1174. *Memorials of the Cathedral and Priory of Christ at Canterbury* (1912) (Woodruff and Danks) contains Erasmus' late visit to Becket's shrine, its destruction and Culmer's iconoclasm in 1642.

History and archaeology

Canterbury Archaeological Trust's first five volumes on specific areas in the *Archaeology of Canterbury* series are for specialists, but popular publications such as *Pilgrim Inns*, Tim Tatton-Brown's *Canterbury in Domesday Book* (1987) and *Three Great Benedictine Houses* (1984) and Frank Panton's *Canterbury's Great Tycoon* (1990) are available from the Trust's office at 92a Broad Street, Canterbury CT1 2LU.

Alec Detsicas' *The Cantiaci* (1981) covers the Belgic and Roman periods. Nicholas Brooks' *The Early History of the Church at Canterbury* (1984) is indispensable up to 1066. Tim Tatton-Brown's contribution on the Anglo-Saxon Towns of Kent is in D. Hooke (ed.) *Anglo-Saxon Settlements* (1988). David Knowles' *Bare Ruined Choirs* vividly describes, among others, the dissolution of Canterbury's religious houses. Brian Hart's *The Canterbury and Whitstable Railway* (1991) is the fullest and most recent study. Niall Rothnie's *The Baedeker Blitz* (1992) includes Canterbury among other German targets in 1942 and Graham Martin's *From Vision to Reality* (1990) chronicles fully the first quarter century of the University of Kent at Canterbury, in a balanced and thought-provoking manner.

Buildings

John Newman's *North-east and East Kent* (3rd ed. 1983) in the *Buildings of England* series covers all the city's interesting buildings. Canon Derek Ingram Hill's *Canterbury Cathedral* (1986) is a lively and comprehensive introduction. Margaret Sparks' English Heritage guide to *St Augustine's Abbey* (1988) is valuable, as is her *Recovery and Excavation of the St Augustine's site 1844–1984* (1984). She has also edited the forthcoming Cathedral history and, with Nigel Ramsey, produced *The Image of St Dunstan*

122

(1988). David Edwards' *History of the King's School, Canterbury* (1957) is the standard work. For specific buildings, consult the indexes of *Archaeologia Cantiana*, the journal of the Kent Archaeological Society.

People

Edward Carpenter's *Cantuar* (1988) introduces many of the first hundred Archbishops. D.H. Farmer's *Oxford Dictionary of Saints* (1987) is full of information on dedications and the lives of Canterbury saints. Bede's *Ecclesiastical History* (Everyman 1963) tells inimitably the story of St Augustine's mission and after. Wraight and Stern's *In Search of Christopher Marlowe* had a new edition in 1993 for the fourth centenary of his death. Brian Stewart lets *Thomas Sidney Cooper R A* (1983) speak through his pictures. Brown, Hutchinson and Irwin's *Written City* (1990) is an anthology of descriptions by eye-witnesses and visitors to the city from Chaucer to Virginia Woolf. John Peters' *A Family from Flanders* (1985) records one immigrant family's fortunes.

The Kentish Context

Produced for the Kent County Council in 1966, Frank Jessup's *Kent History Illustrated* is still useful for its Canterbury and East Kent material. Canterbury in an archaeological and geographical perspective appears in Drewett, Rudling and Gardiner's *The South-East to AD 1000* (1988) and in Brandon and Short's *The South-East from AD 1000* (1990). An economic and sociological study of Canterbury and Kent from 1500 to 1640 features in Peter Clark's *English Provincial Society* (1977). Alan Everitt's *Continuity and Colonisation: the evolution of Kentish Settlement* (1986) and his earlier *The Community of Kent and the Great Rebellion* (1966) are full of insights into Canterbury's place in the county, further discussed by C.W. Chalklin in *Seventeenth-Century Kent* (1978).

The Visitors' Centre in St Margaret's Street or the Canterbury Centre in St Alphege Lane have lists of interesting locally produced pamphlets on aspects of the city's history or its building and planning problems.

I hope that this book may prompt people to go back to Chaucer's *Canterbury Tales*, Marlowe's plays and poetry, Foxe's *Book of Martyrs* and the great antiquarians, Somner, Hasted and Gostling and T.S. Eliot's *Murder in the Cathedral*. Kenneth Pickering's *Drama in the Cathedral: Festival Plays 1928–48* (1985) puts this last work in context.

Glossary

Roman

amphora A large Roman imported wine or oil jar of varied shape sometimes reused for cremation.

cavea The arched passageway on the rear curve of a Roman theatre giving access to the banked seating.

insula (ae) The roughly square areas between the street-grid of planned Roman towns.

mortarium A wide-rimmed Roman grinding dish with grit-set interior for food preparation.

pilae Stacks of brick or tile supporting the raised floors of Roman heated buildings.

potin coins Gauls used an alloy of tin, copper, lead and zinc for minting coins which remained current in Roman Durovernum.

spatha A long, two-edged, broad, blunt-ended cavalry sword used by Roman auxiliary soldiers. The legionary *gladius* was a short, pointed, stabbing sword.

Saxon

Cantwaraburh 'Kent-peoples'-stronghold'. Pre-Roman Belgic immigrants adopted the 'Cant' prefix, retained in Durovernum Cantiacorum. The Jutish war-band, of mixed origin, also became adoptive men of Kent.

cathedra The official chair of a bishop or archbishop giving a cathedral where it stood its name. Pronouncements on faith and morals were made '*ex cathedra*'.

Chi-Rho The Greek ☧ or monogram of Christ appearing on Canterbury's *ligula* and spoons in a hoard *c.* 410.

ligula A pointed implement to scoop ointment from Roman jars.

narthex Western antechamber in early churches where processions often assembled, which was reserved for women and new converts.

porticus More akin to an aisle than a porch, found north and/or south of early Saxon churches, as at Canterbury.

Villae Regales Large estates worked by dependent labour with accommodation for the entourage of an itinerant Jutish king, where he consumed their produce, settled legal disputes and held court.

Medieval

advowson The right of presentation to a church living, retained by lay founders of new churches or donated to religious houses, a practice discouraged by bishops.

demesne The home farmland of a feudal lord originally cultivated directly. These were increasingly leased out by the fifteenth century, especially by monastic lords.

'Observants' The rival attractions of charitable or educational work and contemplative simplicity caused tension before the late medieval split between Regular and Observant Franciscans. The latter, including the Canterbury house, retained popular sympathy and suffered greatly from Henry VIII.

prebendary A post-Reformation Canon at a cathedral, whose stall was often named from the prebendal lands from which his income or prebend came.

secular canons/Augustinians Groups of priests lived communally under various rules before Canons Regular following the Rule of St Augustine of Hippo were founded in 1059. Lanfranc's canons at St Gregory's were regularized by the first Augustinian Archbishop in 1123.

'translation' St Thomas's body was moved to its new shrine in July 1220, providing a second anniversary feast to his December martyrdom, in better pilgrim weather. Thereafter shrine offerings reflected these regular peaks.

Architectural
ashlar Squared blocks of stone as distinct from flint or rubble.

barbican An outer work adding to the defences of the main gate of a castle.

crown-post/king-post From the tie-beam spanning a timber building where the roof began, a king post rose to the apex of the rafters; a crown post only to the collar beam which formed an isosceles triangle with the apex.

double-jettied Extra upstairs space, structural stability and protection for projecting windows was provided by extending first and subsequent floor beams beyond the wall line on the front and/or side elevations of timber-framed buildings.

English bond Early brick walls had alternating rows of end-on 'headers' and lengthways 'spacers' whereas **Flemish bond** alternated 'headers' and 'spacers' in each row, or 'course'.

hall house A hall with central hearth usually separated from the side-set entrance passage by a screen. To either extremity could be added a private 'solar' on an undercroft or workshop and garret. 'Kentish' hall-houses had two-storey projecting ends with the hall recessed under a common roof. Arch braces supported the overhanging central eaves.

machicolation(s) Holes through which hot or cold liquids and/or small stones could be poured on attackers, usually above gates.

merlon(s) The upstanding portions along the top of a defensive or 'crenellated' wall.

solar The private chamber of the head of the household and his ladies. It was usually the first room to have a fireplace and often a bay window for good sewing light.

Other
Sailing hoy A single-masted coastal vessel, fore and aft rigged, of about 20 to 50 tons. It stopped for cargo or passengers when hailed from the shore by 'Ahoy'.

Index

(Page numbers in **bold** refer to illustrations)